WHITE KNUCKLES

WHITE KNUCKLES

Getting Over the Fear of Flying

Layne Ridley

Doubleday & Company, Inc.
Garden City, New York
1987

Library of Congress Cataloging-in-Publication Data

Ridley, Layne.
  White knuckles.

  1. Fear of flying. I. Title.
RC1090.R53   1987   616.85′225
ISBN 0-385-23793-6
Library of Congress Catalog Card Number: 86-24397

For Bob Ridley, with my love and thanks

Contents

Contents

Preface

My timing is either very bad or very good.

At the end of 1984, about the time I first decided to write this book, no passenger traveling in the United States on a major air carrier jet had died in a plane crash for over two years. The international record, although not quite as pristine, was still the best since jet travel began. Considering the fact that these records were being set during years when more people than ever before were flying, I could look forward to quoting some pretty magnificent odds in favor of any airline passenger's safe and uneventful transit.

The odds are still impressive. But they began to sound a little hollow against what happened in 1985, the deadliest year, by far, in civil aviation history. One catastrophe followed another all year. By the end, 2,109 people worldwide had died in thirty-one accidents, counting both regularly scheduled and charter flights.[1] Granted, "only" two of those crashes involved major U.S. carriers (the New Year's Day Eastern crash in Bolivia and the August crash in Dallas of a Delta L-1011), but that fact became a minor footnote as month after month, reports of the next airline disaster seemed to share headlines with investigations of the last.

Right along with other stories nearly as alarming—budget cuts at the Federal Aviation Administration, huge fines levied against major airlines, overworked air traffic controllers, the effects of deregulation. The shocking series of terrible accidents raised new questions and dramatized old ones. Virtually every aspect of air safety was undergoing intense, critical examination.

Maybe I didn't pick such a great time to tell people not to be afraid of flying.

After 1985, even people who had flown for years without a moment's trepidation caught themselves listening for funny noises. And people like me, who had flown for years without a moment's *peace,* were feeling miserably confirmed. See—there *is* something to be afraid of.

Which is why I wanted more than ever to write this book. If you were afraid to fly before 1985, events since then might be enough to keep you stranded on the ground forever. Or, when the time comes that you just about *have* to fly to get where you need to go (and the time just about always comes eventually in the present world of far-flung obligations), you may be even more implacably convinced that you are strapping yourself in for certain death.

You do not need the aggravation.

I was a fearful—make that chokingly petrified—flier for years. You will never hear from *me* that there's nothing to be afraid of. As far as I'm concerned, the world is divided into two kinds of people: normal, intelligent, sensitive people with some breadth of imagination, and people who aren't the least bit afraid of flying. The latter are usually all right otherwise. In fact, you usually don't notice anything is the matter with them until you get them up in a plane and see that dumb, vacant look on their faces. Then you find out a person you thought you knew is mysteriously unable to register the difference between being in the air and being on a bus.

This book was written for normal, intelligent, sensitive people with some breadth of imagination who would like to be able to fly with reasonable calm. That's all. Just get where they are going, on a plane, without pounding heart, wracked nerves, and white knuckles.

We have all, to our sorrow, seen some appalling flying-related sights in recent years, and heard some frightening questions. My purpose is to give you facts and ideas to weigh in the balance. Especially if you have always found one plane that crashes much easier to believe than the millions of planes that don't.

WHITE KNUCKLES

1

The Perfectly Sensible Fear of Flying

You know the odds are overwhelmingly in your favor. Millions to one, right? You know that at any airport, any hour of the day, you can see thousands of people getting off planes, rumpled but reasonably unscathed. Nobody else on any flight you've ever been on seems to be the least bit nervous. For years you have been told that flying is safer than driving around the block. You try to keep that in mind as your plane barrels down the runway, but when it leaves the ground, all those puny reassurances take off with it, and once again, there you are, flying through the air and scared to death.

I was sure I would never get over it. The more I flew, the worse it got. I hated the sounds—the drones that change to grumbles that ominously change to whines. I hated the sensation—like being dangled in an armchair off the top of a skyscraper. And I hated the suspense—is something going to happen now? Or now? Or *now?*

I pretended very hard to be completely nonchalant. No use dressing for success if you're going to cringe like a whipped dog for two hours. I used to tell myself that since I was going to die, I should attempt to die with some style. Smile a world-weary smile of annoyance when the engines exploded. Raise one eyebrow when the wing cracked off. I tried to look bored. It's hard to look bored when you are jerking in your seat at every bump as if you have been slipped twenty volts. So I tried to look bored, but energetic.

When I finally could not, possibly, under any circumstances, sit there one second longer just *waiting* for the flaming plunge, I'd pat back a little yawn, stroll to the bathroom—and make deals with God. In the toilets of major airlines I have fervently renounced every sin in my life, mortal or venial, often including ones I had been dispatched by my employers expressly to commit. Lord, just let me get down alive. Kill me any other way but this.

That much faking, jumping, clutching, and pleading is pretty strenuous. At the end of each flight, I felt like a marathon runner staggering across the finish line. Rubbery-legged, but jubilant. I had, unexpectedly, escaped with my life.

My friends got a big kick out of this little phobia. I overheard a business associate telling someone once that flying with me was "hilarious." I've been sternly lectured: "There's nothing wrong with the plane, now let go of my arm and stop being such a baby." I've been cruelly teased: "Gee, I don't think I've ever heard an engine do *that* before." People were always assuring me that they flew all the time and nothing had happened to them. I, of course, knew that nothing would happen to *them*. The airline disaster I was worried about was out there getting ready to happen to *me*.

I reached the inescapable conclusion that I had a completely irrational fear. I was terrified of one of the most routine operations of my century. I was crazy.

After years of being humiliated by friends and strangers alike with the smug assertion that "flying is safer than driving around the block," I finally checked the numbers. I felt even crazier.

Flying is safer than driving around the block, all right. Mile for mile, it's about 29 times safer than driving *anywhere*.[1] Congressman Norman Mineta, the Chairman of the House Aviation Subcommittee, observed, "Those of us who have been around safety statistics long enough eventually get to the point where we are more nervous driving to the airport, and then when we get there and take our seat on the airplane we relax and feel more secure."[2] Of the over 44,000 people who died on American streets and highways in 1985, almost 8,000 were pedestrians, which means that in the United States almost eight times as many people died by *walking,* during a single year, than have died in passenger jet crashes in the last eleven years.[3] Actually, a jetliner about the size of a 727 would have to crash without survivors every day, seven days a week, to kill as many people as earthbound motor vehicles do in a year. Thus car insurance costs a fortune and flight insurance costs a dollar.

Flying is also safer than staying at home. For one thing, if you're worried about planes crashing, a lot more of them will fly *over* you in your lifetime than you'll ever be *on.* For another, at least 20,000 people are killed every year, and 80,000 more are permanently disabled, in accidents right in their own homes. Not that you're much better off at work, where another 11,500 accident fatalities occur during the year. I guess you could try moving in with your relatives, although relatives (mostly spouses) kill each other off at the rate of 7,000 or so homicides annually, not even counting those who are annoyed to death. In fact, I'm not really trying to widen your circle of fears here, but compare a commercial airline passenger's approximately 1-in-3-million chance of dying during the flight with your approximately 1-in-133 chance of being murdered sometime in your life. One in 10,000 that it happens *this year.* Sort of makes a person want to *live* on an airliner. Except then you would miss your 1-in-260,000 chance of seeing a starter pitch a complete perfect baseball game.[4]

In 1985 the number of people who died in plane crashes involving big jets flying scheduled flights by American carriers around the world was 195. During all of 1980, 1981, 1983, and 1984 it was 0. Since 1974, out of over *sixty million* regularly scheduled American passenger flights, in this country less than twenty have ended in fatal accidents.*[5,6]

So, we can agree flying is pretty spectacularly safe. But some of us don't care. About 40 million of us.[7]

Twenty-five million Americans are so afraid to fly that they make every effort not to do it at all. Another 15 million or so fly if they have to, but are anywhere from uncomfortable to utterly panicked the whole time. Most of them aren't pathetic little misfits, either. Tom Bunn, a pilot and director of the Seminars On Aeroanxiety Relief (SOAR) pro-

---

* Some people love statistics and some people hate them. The references for the numbers I've used here, together with a few additional statistics, appear, for those who love them, in the Notes section, tucked out of the way of those who've probably already had quite enough.

gram, has worked with hundreds of *extremely* fearful fliers. Although his "students" vary widely in age, profession, background, and almost every other way, he says, "Two things are invariably true about people who have real difficulty with flying. They're always highly intelligent, and they're always extremely imaginative." Fear of flying is one of the commonest fears reported to the Phobia Society of America (the *most* common is agoraphobia, or fear of leaving the house. You think *you're* extremely imaginative).

I didn't report my fear to the Phobia Society. You probably haven't called yours in, either. Relative to the huge numbers who are suffering, only a tiny minority of fearful fliers will take special classes or seek professional help. Most will just stay off planes, resigning themselves to the bus, or the train, or to marathon cross-country drives, or to staying at home. The rest of us would be delighted to stay off planes, but some necessary journey or other keeps forcing us onto the horrible contraptions, so we resign ourselves to white knuckles. In a world where flight is so commonplace, the fear of flying is not a very fashionable condition. Fear of intimacy or fear of success are practically badges of honor, but *flying?* Flying is safe. Everybody does it. This is the Jet Age. You're crazy.

You may be crazy. They let anybody into bookstores. But fear of flying is not crazy. Nor is it stupid, cowardly, or ridiculous. It isn't crazy in a year when there are no crashes any more than it is in a year when there are thirty.

Because how *safe* flying is has absolutely nothing to do with how *scary* it is.

For you, for me, for millions of people, the experience of flying is dramatically different from the reality of flying.

Fear may be an irrational response to being transported on a sophisticated and highly reliable vehicle, maintained and operated by experts and specialists at every level, who are following procedures so precise, so carefully tested, and so standard that even small discrepancies are unusual.

Fear, however, is a perfectly sensible response to being propelled with great force into the air and suspended mysteriously at a terrific height, utterly at the mercy of a roaring machine you know nothing about, and with no way out but way, way down.

No one tells you what's happening. The "information" cards are likely to feature cartoons of people inflating boats and sliding down ladders, while looking no more alarmed than if they were riding the rides at Disney World. The pilots don't tell you anything. *They* know everything is okay. They're driving. A pilot in a chatty mood might tell you when you've reached 35,000 feet. Which always used to make me wonder what light indicating mechanical failure was flashing while he wasn't paying attention. The flight attendants don't tell you anything beyond how to buckle your seat belt and pull the string on your oxygen mask. Who can really blame them? Nobody even listens to that little speech. Nobody, that is, except people like you and me, sitting there miserably convinced that if we ever really needed any of that stuff, it would be too late.

Now, the other passengers on the plane don't have much idea what's keeping the whole production aloft, either. So, why aren't *they* scared? Beats me. They just mindlessly expect to land eventually, just like they expect Channel 4 to come on when they punch "4." I will not speculate on what accounts for such dullness of spirit, but who's being irrational here?

Modern man, woman, and child have enormous blind faith in technology. We don't have time to figure out *why* all the hardware in our life works. Just show us the buttons to push. This faith seems reasonable enough in the case of jet flight. Unfortunately, in the case of jet flight, about 40 million of us don't *have* the faith. Maybe we don't need to fathom the inner workings of our personal computers, but there seems to be rather more at stake seven miles in the air. Since we don't know anything for sure except that we are definitely airborne, our superior imaginations are glad to take over. If you don't *know* that that terrible rumbling noise is the flaps going down, you can be forgiven for imagining that it is, instead, the plane going down.

A fear of plane crashes isn't so crazy, either. We read the story of a plane crash with terrible fascination. The images are harrowing and indelible. Any explanations given seem flimsy against the wreckage and the dead and the slightest of chances.

All the planes that do not crash, that we get on every day, look just like the one that did. When we fly we are doing something no more extraordinary than what the passengers that day were doing—going to a business meeting, visiting relatives, taking a vacation. Their odds were good, too.

You have a perfectly sensible fear of an activity you actually know very little about. An activity that *feels* a lot scarier than anything else you do. Say what you will, looking out a window from 35,000 feet is a lot jazzier than standing around the water cooler. And you have a vivid recollection of some pretty grisly photographs involving what was left of a vehicle practically identical to the one you are expected to board without qualms.

You're not crazy. You're too smart for your own good.

Now, you have several options.

You can never fly. If you never fly, you can never crash. You still have to worry about that plane crashing into your house, of course, but you will never have to worry about overbooking.

You can drink. Or take drugs. I've done this myself. After a couple of drinks, I still thought we were going to die, but I didn't care so much. Occasionally, after a couple more, I started finding it very merry, all of us plunging to our deaths, drinking lukewarm wine, eating cold chicken, like a little picnic before the firing squad. I once flew in a tiny private plane from Houston, Texas, to Hilton Head, South Carolina, in a peaceful Valium fog. I would come to, every once in a while, to hear the pilot (who was a college student and part-time cocktail waitress) asking the copilot (her boyfriend, my husband's golfing buddy) if he could make out the name on the water tower so they could figure out where we were. My eyes would roll back in my head and I'd pass out again. Frankly, I am still inclined to believe that flying long distances in a vehicle that is little more than a subcompact with wings, piloted by a golfer's girlfriend, is best done under sedation.

However, the anesthesia system has drawbacks. If you are flying on business, for instance, and have to actually *do* something when you land, it may spoil your image somewhat to fall down during your presentation.

You can go on being terrified. There's definitely something to be said for this option. If you are properly terrified, surviving a routine flight can have the same illuminating force as an escape from a burning building or the news that there was a mix-up over in X-ray and you are not going to die in six weeks after all. Takeoff can be an experience not unlike religious conversion or front-line combat: all the incidentals float away, and your life is revealed in its starkest outlines. Really scared people can come up with some wonderful personal revelations that would probably never have occurred to them on the subway. They resist falling asleep because they discover they are holding up a DC-10 by sheer force of will. Long-forgotten childhood prayers come back to them word for word. A graduate of U.S. Air's Fearful Flyers' course told me he now found flying very disappointing. When he was terrified, landing used to fill him with profound exultation. Now he just had to get off the plane and go to work.

If you have to fly a *lot,* of course, all that regularly scheduled blind terror is going to wear you down. You may also run out of things to promise. I'd already forsworn everything that made my life worth living in the first *month* of my commuter marriage. I began to feel a little sheepish when I got down to promising to pay my bills on time. Didn't seem like much to offer for a hundred and fifty lives.

You can undergo psychoanalysis, and if you think your fear of flying is related to infantile vertigo brought on by subtle early parental pressure and is merely one manifestation of your chronic inability to make mature psychological adjustments, you probably should. You'll get to the bottom of the problem eventually, but don't plan to do any flying for about five years, at which time you may not be able to afford to go anywhere.

I also met a woman who said her fear of flying had been completely cured by acupuncture. Don't ask.

You can gut it out. You can offer it up. You can go on doing whatever you've been doing to force yourself to fly. You can go on driving endlessly into the night.

Or you can decide you're tired of dancing a phobia around, and put yourself, for just a hundred pages or so, in my no-longer-trembling hands. It's the easiest, least expensive way, and if by chance you *are* crazy (or I am), I've provided some ideas about what you can try next (in the Appendices at the back of the book).

No matter how terrified you are, no matter if you've never flown, no matter if you've always been afraid of flying or just mysteriously developed the phobia one day last spring when you idly looked out the window and realized how *high* you were, no matter how silly you think your particular fear is (Is it sillier than being afraid of getting sucked down the airline toilet? It is?)—if you are not a raving lunatic, you can change the way you experience flying.

I got over my fear of flying without psychiatrists, classes, clinics, hypnosis, or drugs—and if I did, you can. If I did, *anybody* can. As you have no doubt gathered, I practically was a raving lunatic. Every time I started that long last march from the gate (my earthly life) to the plane (eternity).

You only have to do three things. They are probably not half as strenuous as the psychological maneuvers you use now to make yourself fly. And they won't take a fraction of the time you spend on trains or buses getting *out* of making yourself fly.

1. *You have to find out what you're afraid of.* Before you hurt my feelings by answering, "Flying, you idiot," give me a chance. I know I said fear of flying is perfectly rational, and a good part of it is. But let us admit at the outset that we have allowed our imaginations to do some embellishment. What else are imaginations for? A plane flight has become such a psychological moment of truth for many fearful fliers that they're way past being afraid of anything so simple as a plane crash. The final part of this chapter is about how to untangle your rational misgivings about flying from your semihallucinatory ones.

2. *You have to get enough factual information to remove the rational basis for your fear.* You're mostly scared by what you *think* is happening, or might happen, or could just barely, conceivably, possibly happen, on a typical airline flight. In chapters 2 through 5, I'm going to tell you what really *is* happening. And I won't leave out the exceptions, either. I'm going to give it to you as straight as I can, even to the point of talking about some recent plane crashes (by then you'll be able to take it). I have researched this book with the insatiable spirit of a true neurotic. I wanted *proof* flying was safe, the kind of proof only the terrified require. I never got enough proof (I'd need an angelic visitation to get *enough* proof), but I found out a surprising thing. There really isn't that much to be afraid of. You may decide otherwise, but at least you'll be deciding on the factual merits of the case.

3. *You have to know how to prepare for and get fearlessly (well, comfortably, at least) through your next flight.* For immediate terror, we need immediate relief. After you've found out enough facts so that

plane trips are no longer flights into the unknown, all you will need are some specific strategies: simple steps you can take before and during your flight so that you can relax and, dare I suggest, enjoy.

Please do not be alarmed. I know that most how-to books always sooner or later come to some dismaying regimen to be followed *every day,* some step-by-step process that you would have to quit your job and leave your family in order to follow completely. Chapter 6 is not going to be like that. Everything in Chapter 6 is easy, and that word "easy" is coming to you from a woman who thinks aerobic dancing is blatantly sadomasochistic.

WHAT ARE YOU AFRAID OF?

There are two kinds of fear (all right, I'm not Sigmund Freud, but see if this doesn't sound right). One kind is directly connected to a danger in the outside world, like when, say, someone is pointing a gun at your temple. Or you wake up and smell smoke. Or you're jogging by the Joneses' house and you discover their Doberman has slipped his chain.

The other kind is mainly connected with a danger inside your head. Fears like this range from the indispensable ones that sustain civilization, such as fear of embarrassment, to the loony ones like fear of your neighbors bombarding you with lethal invisible laser rays. This kind of fear may have a tiny root in reality, but its true medium is the imagination, where it blossoms mightily.

Fear of flying is usually a perfect hybrid.

On one hand, most people who are afraid to fly are responding directly to what they clearly perceive as external dangers: extreme height, mysterious sounds, unfamiliar sensations, the logical inconsistency of the whole damn operation.

On the other hand, those same people may not be scared at all under other conditions even more objectively frightening. A World War II combat veteran told me he was much more terrified by the idea of flying than he had been as a young man going off to war. Athletes in sports where injury is commonplace, actors who perform easily before thousands of strangers, women who have faced with perfect equanimity the travail of childbirth, and millions of other people who deal effectively with just about every other aspect of their lives in this dangerous world

have found themselves reduced to helpless terror at the thought of riding in an airliner. It takes a lot more than a little shaking and rattling to
scare people like that. Or people like you. Something else is going on.

Flying has become for many people a pivot on which lots of other
fears, neuroses, misgivings, and various shreds of free-floating angst
revolve. Even the most routine flight can turn into an emotional
minidrama. The stage is set with everything necessary: danger (the horror of a crash is much more compelling than the notion of its improba-
bility); constraint (once you take off, you can't change your mind or
avoid the issue); and mystery (there's not much room for your imagination to work in a taxi, but your imagination can expand through every
crack and crevice of a plane). Lights, camera, action.

Think about this for just a minute. When you say you are afraid of
flying, what are you *really* afraid of? I don't anticipate any galvanizing
psychological breakthroughs, here. But at any time during a flight, you
should be able to make a pretty fair guess: is something scary happening
out in the world, or is something scary happening in my mind? Have we
got a scary plane ride going on here, or a scary metaphor?

Are you afraid of being out of control?

Rats, I'm told, can take a lot of punishment in the lab without losing
weight or fur or their little rat minds, as long as they know when the
shocks are coming, and as long as there's a lever they can press to
interrupt the shock, even for a second. They just don't like being helpless.

Who does? Some people never at any other time in their lives feel
quite as helpless as they do on a plane. Nothing at all is required of
them. No way to know when or if the shocks are coming, no lever to
press in any case. Sometimes even the illusion of control is better than
none, resulting in an I-am-responsible-for-all-these-lives approach to
flying: somehow it is *my* prayers, *my* watchfulness, *my* mental attitude
that will keep the plane up—or *my* sins that might bring it down.

You probably have a great deal of experience delegating responsibility
to others, and the information in this book about the system and individuals to whom you are delegating the operation of your plane should

ease your mind a little. Nevertheless, that aspect of your flight will remain out of your direct control. What you *can* control, though, is the way you respond to the situation, an effort which should keep you busy enough not to mind that they won't let you fly the plane.

Are you afraid because you feel trapped?

Because you can't get off once you've gotten on? It's true you probably could, while enroute, if worse came to worst, get off or out of almost any other conveyance. Not without considerable trouble, of course, but less trouble than getting off a flying plane.

But how often does worse come to worst? When's the last time you had to make the bus driver pull over for an unscheduled stop because you ABSOLUTELY HAD TO GET OFF?

Only planes (and New York City subways) seem to elicit this intense sensation of being sealed up and past the point of no return. Although a plane isn't much more physically confining than most other public transportation, you really are sealed up and couldn't even breathe very well if the seals broke. So there's nowhere to run. For some people, what brings worse to worst is that there's also no place to hide. Your exposure to caprice is, for the time being, absolutely fixed. These days a chemical cloud, a murderer in a fast-food restaurant, a pain-reliever poisoner, a religious fanatic from an unpronounceable sect, God knows what else, may intersect with us at any time through no fault of our own. Getting on a plane is the only time people feel they have deliberately, irrevocably put *themselves* in harm's way.

Do you have a guilty conscience?

I am quite sure there are more than 40 million guilty consciences in this country, but something about being in a plane makes a lot of people feel like sinners in the hands of an angry God. Flights seem to be opportunities for self-recrimination that just can't be passed up, probably because flying *feels* so momentous to a person who has no idea what perfectly mundane mechanical operations are taking place. A strong impression is created that God is lifting you semi-miraculously into the sky, and, while He's got you there, He might take this opportunity to review your records.

Have you, by chance, seen one too many movies?

Other than takeoff and landing shots to suggest travel, about the only times you see much of a plane in the movies or on television is when something terrible is about to happen on one. Terror at 30,000 feet. Destination disaster. Room for one more. Fate is the hunter. Once you get it into your head that while everyone else on your flight is drinking or sleeping *you* can see the camera narrowing down on the wires sparking in the hydraulic system, the image is hard to shake.

Personally, my real-life airline flights have had about as much resemblance to the movies as my real-life love life. However, we have all been patiently taught by movies and television that (1) if you tell someone you're going to stop flying after today, you're dead, (2) if the person next to you assures you that a crash is absolutely impossible, everybody aboard is dead, and (3) just when things are going smoothly, disaster will strike.

But the most terrifying disaster movie of all is the one you lovingly script, produce, star in, and watch, over and over, in mental 3-D. And that particular screen adventure you can do without.

Does superstition have anything to do with your fear?

I never had to worry about this because I carry my special orange rabbit's feet, but I can sympathize with you, especially since tragic irony seems to be the main theme of reportage about plane crashes: the husband whose last remark to his wife was "The weather doesn't bother these babies", the erring pilot who was just written up in the airline's magazine for reliability, the survivor who changed seats at the last minute. No wonder we blanch when a loved one seeing us off at the gate says, "Come on, it's not as if we'll never *see* each other again, we'll get everything straightened out on Wednesday." Flying standby always posed a particular dilemma for me: Was I going to be the standby passenger who barely made it *onto* the doomed flight, or the one who barely escaped by being bumped?

I have a suspicion that even the fact that you bought and are reading this book may make you a little queasy. Well, how do you think I feel? I can see the headlines: WOMAN WHO WROTE BOOK ON FEAR OF FLYING DIES IN FIERY CRASH. I'm taking a bigger chance than you are, rabbit's feet or no.

How's your sex life?

I only bring it up because the idea of flying is widely believed to have sexual resonances. Flying in dreams, for instance, is supposed to have a sexual symbolism; some ace pilots are said to be making a subconscious substitution of flying for sex; planes themselves have been identified as phallic symbols; and there's something about fairy tales too disgusting to relate. I suppose someone—Erica Jong, for instance—might make the observation that clearing up one's fear of flying might clear up problems in other departments. Frankly, I don't want the responsibility.

Are you in the Dangerous Decade?

I don't mean the eighties; we're just about out of those. I mean did your difficulties with flying start between the ages of twenty-five and thirty-five? If so, you are, at least in this respect, absolutely typical. Two possible explanations are proffered for this phenomenon. One, many phobias begin after a major life event, for example marriage, divorce, the death of a parent, a change of (or even a particularly successful turn in) a career, or, perhaps most commonly, the birth of a child. Since age 25–35 is typically such an eventful time in a person's life, plenty of opportunities arise to shake your general view of life, and, possibly, afflict you with a fear you're not even aware is related.

And second, many people are quite surprised to find themselves actually turning thirty or thirty-five. The thought often occurs to them for the first time that other events heretofore considered unlikely might also be possible, such as dying. Most of the time they manage to ignore this new consideration. Flying reminds them. Not very gently, either. Sometimes refusing to fly becomes, in Captain Tom Bunn's word, a "talisman." Maybe if they just stay out of planes, everything will be all right.

Actually, if you were on a carefully thought-out campaign not to die at *all,* the next item on your agenda after "Radically change eating habits" would be "Arrange to travel everywhere by air."

But perhaps the most universal and persistent root fear of flying is simple and to the point: *"Something is going to happen to me."* We all know in our hearts that we are the center of the known universe, and that the circumstances of our lives transcend odds because we are destined for some extraordinary fate. Sometimes, on a plane, we feel it might be very extraordinary indeed, like maybe one in a few million.

In a sense, by dramatizing our fear of flying, we are protecting our self-importance. It would diminish us to think: "I am just a statistic, a gnat. Nothing will happen to little old insignificant me. Nothing in my head has anything at all to do with the progress of this plane or any other." How depressing. I'd almost *rather* believe all Heavenly Eyes were on me, and had picked my soul out of all the other thousands in the sky, to weigh in the Scales, to hold up or fling down. Now, *that's* entertainment.

This book will show you the reality of flying. You can use the information here to check out where reality leaves off and your fevered imagination kicks in. Then you can decide which of your cherished secret terrors you would like to keep, and which you can do without.

At the risk of making you despair of a complete cure (and at the risk of inviting you to guess which of the above areas is causing the problem), I will be honest with you and admit that I am still a little afraid of flying. A little irrational flicker persists. The thought still crosses my mind occasionally that my fellow passengers in the gate area all look like photographs of the dead passengers from doomed Flight Whatever-my-flight-number-is.

I guess they all look like they're going to die because they are, but I no longer am so sure it will be today, along with me, in a plane. Now I can usually go the whole flight without remembering to listen to the engines. I can read without squeezing my eyes shut at every bump. I can sleep like a baby. It's a very nice feeling. I can relax because I finally found out what was really happening up there, and my fear doesn't have as much to work with now. By taking the mystery out of flying, I changed a tormenting panic to a mild, almost absentminded little worry, the kind you might have about driving around the block. You know somebody might run into you, but it doesn't seem worth staying home about.

You can get over your fear of flying. And you should. If you're like most people in the latter decades of the twentieth century, you've got a nice collection of fears in every price range, and fear of flying is one you can easily spare. The risk is infinitesimal compared to just about anything else you routinely do, and the benefits are substantial.

That risk will not change after you read this book. But, with any luck, it just won't seem worth staying home about.

What's Really Happening: Reality Check

So let us assume that there is a vivid contrast between what flying *is* (routine transportation on a vehicle that is just a technological extension of an eighteen-wheeler), and what flying *feels* like (voyage of the damned).

In the course of writing this book, I ended up asking dozens of people —everyone who would hold still for it—about the way flying feels to them. I won't characterize my victims as a scientific sample, but the results were about what you would expect. At one end of the spectrum were pilots and other enthusiasts who think flying feels wonderful, it feels like freedom, release, conquest, triumph, sailing through the heavens. I guess there's no accounting for taste.

In the vast middle of the spectrum were those who represent the majority of airline passengers. When I asked them what flight feels like, most looked at me blankly. It doesn't feel like anything. It feels like sitting in a plane going to Baltimore. I don't know how it feels, many said, I usually go to sleep.

Unable to believe, no matter how often I heard it, that anyone could actually hardly notice being propelled at 500 m.p.h. 35,000 feet above firm ground, I would persist. How about turbulence, I would say. Don't you feel the turbulence? Well, they guessed so. A little bump every now and then. A few would search their memories to come up with some example of being reminded that they were airborne. "Once, about ten years ago, we fell so far everyone's trays flew up in the air," a frequent Washington-to-Philadelphia commuter told me.

"My God," I said, "weren't you terrified?" He looked at me as if I had suggested he should be terrified when his car wouldn't start right away. "It was just an air pocket," he shrugged. "It didn't hurt anything. I spilled some beer on my suit, though."

Yes, friends, the numbers of the oblivious are legion. But crouching at the other, pitiful end of the spectrum of people who fly, there are people like us. We can tell you in excruciating detail what flying feels like. It feels like inexplicable plunges and precarious recoveries. It is accompanied by deafening roars and unaccountable whines, and is performed at death-defying heights, with no net. It is controlled by faceless pilots in an invisible chamber. Life rafts coil beneath our seats and oxygen masks threaten to pop out above us. The exits are marked but you cannot use them unless you crash.

What is so scary about a little plane ride? The following is a capsule description, drawn from the sad testimony of panic-stricken fliers, of what a routine plane ride *feels* like to them:

You and the strangers you may die with this morning are strapped into your seats. The beast rumbles to life. It gathers speed, you're hurtling through space and the engines are straining to lift all of you and the plane's gigantic steel bulk into the air. But the engines catch and the plane falters and for a sickening moment it seems likely you will fall back onto the runway.

Then the plane tilts and you are about to tip over. At the last possible second, the first of what you hope will be many miracles occurs. The plane keeps going. It's making a lot of noise, though, the roar seems to be building to a point where the skin must surely crack and the engines rattle off their mountings. Sure enough, the engines *do* begin to fail, they waver, anyway, somebody's fooling with them, but again, for some reason, the plane keeps going. You carefully count the pulses for a little while and are becoming used to the sound of the engines when they slow way down again, not to mention that the whole plane keeps kind of wobbling and faltering and the whines only pulse at a certain rhythm for a few minutes before they mysteriously change—a forgotten wrench, probably, or the wrong kind of fuel, or sabotage.

Then you're flying along on a perfectly clear day and all of a sudden the plane starts bumping a little. Then a lot. Then the seat belt sign goes on. Okay, this is it, all the flight attendants are trying to keep brave faces and go on about their business but you know that any second now you are going to hit the sky equivalent of a pot hole and the entire arcana that is keeping you aloft is going to be unalterably disturbed and you are going to go into a shrieking nosedive. Snuffed out. So young. You never even saw the Pyramids. But then the plane flattens out. Bad sign. Something broke, or else you have entered the always sinister calm-before-the-storm. Getting your hopes up would be deadly. There's no hope, anyway, because you keep feeling little bumps, exactly like bumps that would be caused by a luggage hatch working its way open. Soon it will fly off and you'll be sucked right out of the air, unless the pilot has a heart attack first. When he came over the loudspeaker just now his voice was suspiciously muffled, you couldn't understand a word he was saying, maybe he's sick. Or exhausted. Did he fly all night? The flight attendant's eyes are sort of red, maybe she and the pilot painted the town together all night, it's not impossible, they're far from home, so maybe they—

What's *that?* You definitely detect a different pitch to the rumbling underneath you and the overall whine and you are the only one who hears it, the pilot probably doesn't notice it because he's so used to this, and he's hung over, anyway, but you can hear it and it means only one of two things: something is going wrong with the hydraulic system or something is clogging the fuel lines. Well, three things, an emergency door may be getting ready to fly open. Well, actually, the culprit could be metal fatigue finally culminating in a wing about to spring its bolts, which are no doubt worn to shreds by now, the plane is obviously old, and the mechanics were probably hung over, too, maybe they were out with the pilot and the flight attendant. No, you shouldn't have unchari- table thoughts. God, not *now,* you must think only good thoughts now. Maybe it wasn't drink or loose women, maybe the mechanics were distracted by trouble at home, and made an honest mistake, simply forgot to check everything out. The plane hasn't been vacuumed in a long time, looks like, so maybe the screws and bolts haven't been tight- ened, either, there are a *thousand* things they could have forgotten to check out. Poor souls, they are going to feel really terrible when this crash turns out to be their fault.

Your foot starts to fall asleep. But maybe it's not your foot. Maybe there is a subtle vibration beginning in the floor that means incipient loss of power. Yes, that's exactly the case. At that very moment everything *really* starts to shut down. Okay, it was silly to worry about the luggage hatch but *this* is not your imagination, they really are turning the engines down. Or off. You can tell you're going down. You're still thousands of feet high above the clouds and they are turning off the engines. Must be trouble, or the pilot, unbalanced by the drugs he took to combat the hangover, is going to glide the rest of the way in. Or the engines are losing power and he is frantically pushing buttons and calling Mayday. He tells you over the loudspeaker that "we are beginning our descent." He sounds eerily calm. He's hiding something. Maybe he began by turning the engines down on purpose, but inadvertently turned them down too far, because you can feel very clearly that you are all floating through thousands of feet of empty space, drifting, on the edge of flopping over entirely into free-fall.

The engines speed up. The pilot, clumsy and debauched but brave in his final hour, is trying everything he can think of to save your lives, pull you out of this. The engines slow down again. His maneuvers aren't working. Maybe he's not trying the right ones. Maybe he's new. Why, he's an impostor! He doesn't know what he's doing at all! But you are getting lower, low enough to see the water, now. In fact, low enough so that maybe you're going to miss the runway and land *in* the water. You can't see the runway from here, but you can see a lot of water. Then, because God seems to have overlooked that incident at the office Christmas party after all, you do touch down, and then the plane speeds up but you don't have to worry about falling any more, now all you have to worry about is crashing into the terminal and wiping out your loved ones.

Well, gee, who wouldn't reexamine their Weltanschauung during an experience like *that?* But what is really happening?

First, you must accept the vehicle itself. It is not delicate. A commercial airliner is made of metal alloys designed by an entire department full of metallurgical specialists who know that eventually they are going to have to turn their brainchild over to an entire department of engineering specialists who will rip holes in it, ram guillotine-like blades through it, and drop it onto concrete from towers. The holes cannot spread. The blades cannot penetrate. The smashing cannot do much more than dent it, or else the metallurgists and the engineers have to start all over again. I'll supply you with more details in later chapters about how airplane manufacturers try to think up ways to destroy their products. A plane may seem lyrically fragile to you in the great heavens, but it is an extremely sturdy contraption, about as delicate as a tank. The commercial airliner is like the king of the jungle—very few natural enemies.

When you take off in a plane, you are not only on a wing and a prayer, you are on a vehicle that has been strenuously—to be frank, *compulsively*—tested until it could be pronounced safe under conditions not likely to occur on this planet. Just one small example at this point: in addition to the tests I mentioned above and literally thousands of others, the window prototypes are systematically pelted with dead chickens shot out of a chicken-cannon at 500 m.p.h. You see what I mean? When you are in a commercial airliner, you are in a place like probably no other you are ever in: a place that thousands of people have spent untold hours and untold treasure and untold imagination making safe.

A plane is not delicate. Neither is it mysterious. The only reason it *looks* so mysterious is that air is invisible. If water were invisible, you can bet people would think twice about ocean cruises. Although you may be convinced that you are, by your constant vigilance and force of will, responsible for the plane staying aloft, you must try to understand that it is not you. It is the Bernoulli effect. This will work on your plane even if you fall asleep. Physical laws, thank God for the other people on your flight, are like that. The basic idea of the Bernoulli effect is that the pressure of a moving fluid (or a gas, like air) changes with its speed of motion. The faster the air moves, the lower the pressure.

Airplane wings are designed so that they're curved on top and flat on the bottom. As the wing slices through the air, it divides the stream of air in two, and the top stream, going over the curve, has to move faster than the bottom one. Faster speed, lower pressure. So a controlled imbalance is created, with lower pressure on top and higher pressure on the bottom. This causes lift. The wing is pressed firmly up, bearing you with it into the air. You're being held up as snugly as a piece of salami between two slices of rye. This principle would work just as well on a parked jumbo jet (you would need some pretty big fans). Get enough air blowing over those wings, and the plane could not help but lift.

There is one minor theoretical problem with the Bernoulli effect. It does not explain how planes can fly upside down, which they can, but not with me on them.

Now you must consider what is done with the vehicle. An airliner is an enormously complex machine (a typical one has about 3 million parts), but the fundamental principles are very simple.

And the most important principle to remember about an airplane is that its natural function is straight, level flight. That's what it was designed and built to do, and it could, by its inherent shape, do that without all the machinery.

Without the pilot, even, because if he takes his hands off the controls altogether, a plane which is properly situated in the air will do the only thing a structure balanced as it is can do: return to straight and level flight. How well a specific type of airplane can do this is measured by its "stability," and some are designed for more stability than others. A sensitive, fidgety jet fighter is designed for other qualities. Airliners, in the words of pilot and aviation author Richard L. Taylor, "usually feel as though they're on railroad tracks—very stable, positive, ponderous."[1]

However, I don't feel quite confident without somebody there to notice if the plane perchance wanders to one side of all that air flowing neatly across its wings, so I vote we keep the pilot, and put him in charge of proper situating. And since we additionally need to get into the air in the first place, turn, change altitudes, and eventually land on a designated spot, we really should throw in an engine and some tires and a steering column, and maybe a compass.

All the other countless elaborations are extra—variations on a theme, to enable a sophisticated modern passenger jet to go faster, carry more people, and be operated more safely and reliably than a simple stripped-down model.

But let's take the stripped-down model as an example, for a brief test flight, to get the fundamental operations down before we take off on an airline flight. You fly the plane. I'll pop a few tranquilizers and ride with you.

Four key words: the *lift*, which you know about, is the force opposite
the *weight* of the plane, and the *thrust*, or the power to move forward, is
opposed by *drag*, not only the drag of gravity but the drag of the air as
the plane passes through it. Let's say that you are a lot wealthier than
you look and your stripped-down model has been built with the same
care that goes into a commercial airliner. The aerodynamic profile is
precisely designed for maximum lift, at weights which are several times
heavier than you are ever likely to carry, you have about 3,500 pounds
of thrust (comparable to one of the engines on a fancy corporate jet) at
your disposal and can vary it instantly at will, and the shape and skin of
your plane have been specifically engineered to slip through the air with
the physical minimum of drag. When you get into the air, these four
forces will be in exact equilibrium and you will be in straight, level flight
at a constant speed.

But you have to get *into* the air. So you must arrange to put your
craft into an attitude, at sufficient speed, for lift to occur. You would
like to be able to perform these calculations from scratch, but trigonom-
etry was not your best subject. Not to worry. The manufacturer of your
plane has already figured out exactly how your plane will perform under a wide range of different conditions. So you consult your manual,
and find precise instructions for the angle, speed, control settings, and
every other variable of your takeoff run, your "rotation" (when you lift
the nose off the runway), and your climb. So you can concentrate on
where you're going, I, your trusty copilot, will read this checklist to you
step-by-step.

You follow these instructions and are soon in level flight because
anything shaped like an airplane is required to obey the physical laws of
the universe.

But you can't leave well enough alone, you want to *do* something
while you're up there. Well, there are actually only four things you can
make the plane do. Of course, as anyone who has seen the Blue Angels
knows, the degree to which you do these four things can result in an
infinite number of wonderful variations. I trust you will keep your head
and refrain from such hijinks, or I'll need a barrel of tranquilizers.

You can make the nose go back and forth, to the left or right. But you
don't want to do this, it's called "yaw" and it's nauseating, and one of
the primary functions of the tail is to correct for it, whether you're

yawing on purpose for a cheap thrill or the air is pushing the plane. The vertical stabilizer (the big fixed fin-looking section) and the rudders (the hinged parts attached to it) are there to keep the plane going straight. The entire ingenious tail assembly is beautifully named the *empennage*, and it will come in *très* handy, not only for flying yawlessly straight, but also for the next maneuver.

You can make the nose go up or down, thus varying the "pitch," or attitude, of your plane. The attitude will affect the "angle of attack," which sounds quite colorful, as if we were getting into an aerial dog-fight, but, alas, refers only to the angle at which your wings are attacking the air. The greater the angle, the bigger the lift (within a specific range, of course). You have studied this effect every time you hung your arm out the window of your car on the freeway and found the perfect angle and thrust necessary to keep your hand soaring level. Pointing your plane up or down isn't the only way to affect lift. Speeding up the airflow over the wings will do it, as well.

Control over the pitching movement of a plane is where the rest of your tail (so to speak) comes in. The tail plane, that part below the fin that looks like little wings, is also called the horizontal stabilizer. Say a little gust of wind pushed your wings up. Well, the horizontal stabilizer would lift, too, thus bringing the tail up and restoring level flight. And right behind the horizontal stabilizer are movable surfaces called elevators. Moving them down will force your nose up, and vice versa.

You can roll. I don't mean all the way over, that would be pretty advanced. "Roll" is the general term for putting one wing higher than the other. If you want to turn, you'd better do this. You know how if you're driving along pretty fast and an unidentifiable little animal scurries across the road and stops in the middle to look up at you, and you try to turn the nose of your car sharply to the right to avoid it although God knows why you want to risk your life for a stupid rodent? Remember what happens? The back of your car keeps going straight and you go around in an unpleasant circle. Same with your plane. If you just turn dead right, at the speeds you're flying, you're likely to find yourself heading back the way you came. You wouldn't like aeroskid. Instead, you want to do what race car drivers do. Bank. Lift the wing opposite to the way you want to turn, steer a little bit, and glide off around the invisible banked track you have created. You'll probably use the ailerons on your wings, which can increase lift on one wing and decrease it on the other.

The fourth thing you could do, with practice, is stall, and maintain your stall long enough to crash. You would have to do several things at once, like screwing up the angle of your attitude and eliminating your thrust altogether and forcibly counteracting every move your plane made to automatically correct itself, and ignoring all the warning bells and whistles, and it would take some time—a long time, if the wind was right—to circumvent the natural tendency of wings to fly, but you could probably do it. Between you and me, however, I don't think you have the experience.

So you will have to get down the respectable way, by landing. Landing is a little tricky because you are in effect arguing with the dynamics of the plane, which wants to stay up. So you're going to use the wings that kept you in the air to gradually lower you out of it. On the trailing edge of your wing are flaps, which you can extend to make the wing bigger and give you more lift, and spoilers, which you can raise to "spoil," or slow down, your lift. On the leading edge of your wing are devices aptly named leading-edge devices, another air-deflecting surface which you can lower when you want to slow down enough to stop but keep enough lift to fly right up until then. You have to show the plane who's boss, no stopping until you say so.

You have now penetrated the mysteries of flying an airplane.

Spend a few more hours in a cockpit figuring out where the controls are, and you, too, will be able to fly a plane as well as any college student–cocktail waitress.

If you do not believe me, consider the fact that the Aircraft Owners and Pilots Association has for over twenty years offered a course called the Pinch Hitters Program (Want to sign up? The address is in the back of the book), originally designed mainly for the wives of private pilots.[2] The rationale was based on the fact that if there are only two of you in the plane and the one of you at the controls becomes incapacitated for any reason, the one left awake is going to have more than an academic interest in how long a plane can sustain straight and level flight all by itself. The course consists of four hours of ground training and four hours of flight training, after which a nonpilot can feel reasonably assured that he or she could, in the event of an in-flight emergency, take the controls, contact help on the radio, and land the plane. Richard F. Busch, Jr., the vice president of AOPA's Aircraft and Airmen's Services Department, estimates that fifty thousand people have taken the class. AOPA knows of ten to fifteen people who have had occasion to use their emergency skills in this way. All have safely (if not always smoothly) landed planes after the pilot became suddenly unconscious. The most recent incident he told me about was a woman in Phoenix, whose husband died of a heart attack in the air. She got on the radio, another plane flying in the area heard her requests for help, and the other pilot talked her through to a landing. Mr. Busch allowed as how she bent the nose gear, but the plane was repaired and is still flying.

But let us assume for the present that you would rather let an airline transport you. Good decision.

Here's what you can expect: the same maneuvers you just learned, only bigger.

It's the truth. What you have just read is simplified, I grant you. The dynamics of lift alone are the subject of many thick and learned tomes filled with impenetrable (to me, anyway, and I bet to most pilots) equations. And a four-paragraph course isn't going to approach the depth even of a four-hour one, not to mention the thousands of hours of intensive training and hands-on experience required of an airliner cockpit crew member. To say the captain of an airline flight is just flying a plane is sort of like saying Lee Iacocca is just running an office. But even the most sophisticated passenger jet, a multimillion-dollar marvel of engineering and electronic technology, is performing the same basic maneuvers you went through in your imaginary light plane. Even its pilot, also probably something of a marvel of experience and training, is using the same basic controls to manipulate the same forces: lift, weight, thrust, and drag. But, as I said before, bigger, faster, more precisely, more safely—and a lot noisier. So you should have no trouble recognizing what's going on when you hear it. Here are a few maneuvers to listen for on your next airline flight:

Takeoff. Fearful fliers usually hate takeoff worst of all. That crescendo sounds like it must be building up to something horrendous, but instead it usually builds up to just *hanging.* But getting off the ground in the first place, as you recall, requires more power than any other phase of the flight. The reason it's so noisy is because on a jetliner, each *one* of the two to four engines is generating up to *fifty thousand* pounds of thrust. Modern engines are much quieter than they used to be, an innovation made by the manufacturers not so much to protect our delicate sensibilities as to mollify the militant homeowners around airports who are fond of bringing gigantic noise abatement lawsuits when their peace is disturbed. But that much thrust is hard to keep to a whisper. As soon as you're airborne, though, to keep the noise down, and because the plane doesn't need so much thrust any more, the pilot will ease back on the throttle almost immediately.

You'll also probably hear a pronounced clunk when the landing gear is retracted. It's tucked away so it won't add any drag. The design engineers have made certain that every *bolt* on a plane's skin is flush, to reduce drag, so you know they're not going to leave the *wheels* hanging out.

And you'll probably bank right away, too. The plane has taken off from a runway chosen for the traffic conditions of the day, but you're not necessarily taking off in the precise direction you need to go. Every interval of a plane's route has been carefully laid out in advance, and your plane has to get onto its designated track immediately.

The other operation you may notice is the flaps being retracted. They were extended during takeoff—look out the window; at the back of the wing, you'll see the flaps drawn back into the wing if you're looking at the exact right moment—to make the wing nice and big, for maximum lift. Once you're in the air they'll be needed progressively less and less, and the flap settings will change by minutely described degrees. They won't be needed at full extension again until right before landing.

The sounds of controls, like the flaps, being operated varies with different airliners. Sometimes you'll hear a sort of sliding whine. Sometimes you won't hear a thing. You can't expect them to be *completely* silent, though. A Boeing 747's control surfaces, for example, are so massive that not even the biggest, burliest jet pilot can operate them directly—a hydraulic system (with three complete identical backup systems) is necessary to do the actual pushing and pulling. Still, most of the time during the flight the controls are operating so subtly that you won't be able to hear them. Takeoff and landing are about the only phases where all that machinery might come to your attention.

Climb. Gradually, following its flight plan step-by-step, the plane will ascend in stages to its cruising altitude. Most of the time, this ascent is hardly noticeable. Remember, just pointing the plane up will increase its lift, not even counting the considerable power of the engines. But if there's a lot of traffic in the area, you might notice a few variations in speed before you get to your cruise altitude.

Cruise. I know it *sounds* as though the engine noises keep changing. If you listened very carefully to your electric fan, you could pick out subtle changes in rhythm, too, and I doubt there are as many swirling air currents in your bedroom as there are in the sky through which your plane is passing. Each of your engines is a completely independent system, operating off a completely different power source (which is handy if one has trouble, as we'll see later). So the noises of the two or three or four of them are not, obviously, in absolute sync. When you're up there assiduously counting engine pulses, and could *swear* that the pulses are suddenly out of whack, you should allow for the fact that your ear might have been following one engine, and then got distracted by another. I have tried many times to convince people I know who fly often that I can distinguish minute variations in engine noises. They think I'm nuts. All they hear is one solid monotonous drone. I think that proves their ears are as faulty as their imaginations.

The highways in the sky followed by airliners are just as clearly fixed and marked as the nation's freeways—more precisely, actually, since much shorter intervals are identified. Even the *intersections* are named and numbered. Instead of signs, impractical at that height, the jet route system is designated by radio coordinates. Around the country there are about fifteen thousand VOR (Are you ready? Very-high-frequency Omni-directional Radio-range) radio transmitters, each on a slightly different frequency, emitting beams for each of the 360 degrees around it. You may be traveling from Detroit to Miami but your plane is traveling from one VOR to another, by carefully measured degrees. One more unwieldy acronym: DME (Distance Measuring Equipment). Your plane's route isn't designated just by the numbered radials around the VORs, but also by the distance from each station. These precisely defined one-way horizontal corridors are separated from one another by a thousand feet of space, and above 29,000 feet, by two thousand.

So if you notice you're doing a bit of turning en route, it's so that your plane can stay on its designated track. And if you notice some speeding up and slowing down as you go, it's because the controllers are organizing the traffic on these skyways so that each plane will arrive at each marker in an orderly manner. At home, you've probably done your share of hanging around waiting for a light to change. Planes sometimes have to do the aerial equivalent, but they can't do it *parked*.

Landing. Although I was usually relieved when the approach for landing finally began and I knew earth was at least in *somebody's* sight, I didn't like at all what came next. About a half hour before you're scheduled to land, it may sound very much to you as if all hell is breaking loose. First it feels like you're coming to a screeching halt, then like you're hanging, then like you speed up and slow down way too many times for this activity to be on purpose. I have, of course, been on flights where the descent was hardly noticeable, just a little low rumbling. And if your plane were the only one in the air, all landings would probably be like that, but it's not and they're not.

First, the plane has been going along at a very fast clip, an efficient cruising speed which the crew would like to maintain as long as possible. In fact, you could probably arrive considerably ahead of schedule if the pilot just waited until the plane was right over the airport and then put on the aerial equivalent of the brakes and pointed it down. However, airline flights are not planned for maximum excitement. Instead, the pilot starts slowing down several hundred miles out. That first transition downward will probably be the most noticeable. Remember, you've got very powerful engines and a plane that would just as soon keep flying. As soon as the speed over the wing slows, the lift will gradually decrease, so the flaps will be extended. The objective is to keep the plane relatively level, and moving forward, just at gradually slower speeds and gradually declining altitudes. The engines don't have much to do with things, at this point. The point of an engine is speed, and we don't need any more speed. Every once in a while, the pilot may have to vary the rate at which he's* coming up to the airport, because

---

* You may have noticed that I keep referring to pilots as "he." I couldn't figure out which was more inexcusable: slighting the four hundred or so women who are currently airline pilots, or loading every sentence with "he and/or she." I arrived at a not very satisfactory compromise. But I wish to apologize in advance to women airline pilots everywhere, particularly to Ms. Pamela Stephens, a young woman who looks as if she belongs in a college homecoming queen court but is, instead, a Northwest Orient 747 pilot. Northwest is generally recognized as one of the major airlines with the most stringent rules for pilot qualifications and continuing training. Just one small part of her pilot experience included

the air traffic controller is trying to keep everyone in a certain order. Look out the window. You'll see the control surfaces—the flaps, the spoilers, the leading edge devices—sliding out to balance the plane and slow it down. Somewhere during this period, you'll hear the landing gear coming down. On big jets this generally sounds like the plane is being disemboweled.

And several minutes immediately before landing, you probably will feel the plane really power forward. Gliders can just drift out of the air and plop somewhere in the general vicinity of the planned landing, but airliners must land in a rather more controlled fashion, like for instance straight down the middle of the correct runway, and so the thrust is concentrated in that direction.

And then you'll barrel along the runway as the pilot applies steady pressure to the brakes and then you'll stop.

I hope I haven't spoiled the magic.

ferrying small planes, solo, back and forth across the Atlantic Ocean, a job one of her fellow (male) Northwest pilots told me requires "more guts than *I* have." Every time I use "he" for a pilot, I think of Ms. Stephens and wince—and I want you to do the same thing.

The Horrible Things That Could Happen— and Why They Don't

All right, so maybe the ordinary sounds and sensations aren't as frightening as they seem. Maybe they can be accounted for. It isn't an ordinary flight we're afraid of, though, is it? Aren't there extraordinary things that can happen? In fact, isn't there one particular awful thing that you always think might happen? What if THAT happens?

If THAT happens, you're probably going to ask me for a refund. At *least*. However, most of the THATs we fear so much are astronomically unlikely. Certainly they are unlikely in terms of odds and statistics, as judged against the 5.7 million flights, 380 million passengers, in one year, just on big airlines, just in the United States. Numbers can give you a reasonable perspective—but they can't tell you *why* certain kinds of events are so rare. And there are some very good reasons why.

Presented below is an assortment of fears commonly expressed by scared fliers. Along with each fear are some basic reasons why the particular malfunction, mistake, or catastrophe involved hardly ever happens. But if I found significant exceptions, I might as well warn you, I didn't leave them out.

In fact, I *looked* for them. Fearful fliers dearly love exceptions. I heard* a senior Pan Am mechanic patiently explain the company's

---

* I heard this exchange on a tape of the class, which was generously provided to me by Captain Tom Bunn.

exhaustive maintenance routine to a SOAR class, and when he was finished, before he could get "Any questions?" out of his mouth, a lady in the class began to tell a story about a flight she had been on once that lost two engines and had to turn around and land. "How," she asked in a voice you may remember from "Perry Mason" reruns, "does that square with *your* story?"

The incident had occurred on a different carrier *ten years* earlier, but something in her almost triumphant question made me suspect she had been paying more attention, as the mechanic spoke, to the sounds of that long-ago engine failure than to anything he said.

And to be completely honest, hers is the attitude I took when I checked out the facts in this chapter. The experts I consulted often looked at me strangely when I persisted in asking exactly how often and under what circumstances a particular Bad Thing could happen. "I thought you were writing a book to *reassure* people," I heard more than once. "I want to be accurate," I said, hoping this would impress them with my artistic integrity. What I mostly meant was "I have to fly, too. Let's hear it."

A few of these trepidations are particularly close to my own faint heart, but I happen to think that *all* these fears are perfectly reasonable. As a matter of fact, at some time or other in the history of aviation, almost all of these nightmares have come true—which is the slender thread whereon hangs many a gigantic fear. Fear of flying isn't precisely like most other phobias. If you do any reading at all about phobias, you will immediately notice that somebody somewhere has a debilitating terror of just about every object or circumstance that can be conceived by the overactive human mind. But if you have a phobia about moths, for example (a condition not as rare as you might think), you probably haven't read many accounts of berserk moths killing innocent householders, not in large numbers, anyway. Fearful fliers, on the other hand, watch the newspapers for untoward aviation incidents, searching for that prize exception to convince them flying is dangerous. With about two hundred thousand planes of all shapes and sizes flying in the American skies every day, you're certain to find *something* weird if you're looking.

Unfortunately, in the last couple of years, it sometimes seems you don't have to be looking all that hard, either. As long as there are planes in the sky and reporters on the ground, we're going to hear about every accident, incident, deviation, problem, and suspicion of a problem in great detail. In fact, if you stopped a few average, moderately informed adults on the street, they could probably tell you quite a bit about recent plane crashes and aviation-related news stories—and next to nothing about how planes work the other 99.99 percent of the time.

That's okay for *them*, but unless we smarter-scareder fliers find a way to keep the solid fact of overall safety in sight even when exceptions pop up to block the view, we're sunk. It's hard not to be terrified if you can reel off a dozen reasons why a plane could have trouble and can't think of one good reason why most of them don't.

If my mission were to scare the daylights out of you, I certainly wouldn't have to write a whole *book*. I could do it with one or two well-chosen sentences out of an accident report, or a single photograph. Even the two-word phrase "plane crash" is powerful enough to send shivers down the spine. The image of ordinary, routine, day in and day out absence of danger is much more difficult to convey. So even though I've tried to be realistic about the risks, I trust you already have a keen sense of exceptions, which you no doubt carry onboard every flight. I would like to give you a sense of the rule.

A COMPENDIUM OF WORST FEARS

The plane will run into something.

A building. A mountain. Another plane. Of course, you know this has happened. The 1978 newspaper photo of a Pacific Southwest Airlines Boeing 727 falling near San Diego after colliding with a small Cessna 172 was like a snapshot from one of my nightmares. And on August 31, 1986, an eerily similar disaster in a Los Angeles suburb followed the collision of an Aeromexico airliner and an apparently off-course private plane. It was the eighth midair collision involving loss of life on an airliner since 1939.

We aren't the only ones afraid. In this country, the entire navigational and air traffic control system has been built on the basis of this fear, and new precautions continue to be developed.

Every aircraft flying over 18,000 feet is required by law to be under the direct control of the federal air traffic control system. After the San Diego tragedy, *every* plane flying close to busy terminals was also brought under this rule.† From the moment your airliner rolls away from the gate where you boarded, to the moment it rolls up to the gate to let you off, it is being watched, by human eyes and by computer. A transponder, sort of a miniature radio station onboard the plane, relays information which appears in a little box on the controller's screen. The signals from the transponder, together with the details of your flight plan lodged in the computer in advance, give the controller a great deal of information about your flight. He can call up various items into the little box—the pilot can signal him that way, too, by making the box flash brighter, for instance—but the numbers always contained are your flight number, your altitude, and whether you're ascending, descending, or level.

As you travel, your route will pass through many different sectors, beginning with departure control from the airport tower, then on to one of the twenty regional centers around the country, and finally to another tower for approach control. Each segment of your flight is further divided, so that each controller along the way will only be monitoring your little box while it's in his or her sector—probably only a matter of fifteen to twenty minutes, since planes travel about 500 m.p.h. while cruising and each sector covers only a few dozen miles.

Here's the crux of the matter: no plane can come within five miles of another in the air. The computer instantly registers as soon as two planes *begin* a course that would eventually bring them within five miles of each other, even if the planes are currently controlled by different sectors. The two little boxes begin to flash brightly on the screen. I've

† Although at this time the investigation into the Aeromexico crash is still incomplete, apparently the private plane involved had violated the controlled airspace around Los Angeles International Airport, an area where the daily traffic of private planes is higher than anywhere else in the country. The accident focused attention on the borders between where private planes can and cannot fly without a controller's permission, since those relatively narrow bands near large airports are the only areas where a small plane is liable to be anywhere near a big plane, even by mistake, unless ground control and the airliner's crew both know about it. As vivid as this recent disaster probably remains in your mind, you can imagine how vivid it is in the minds of air traffic controllers, private pilots, and airline pilots coming into busy airports, so even tighter restrictions on terminal control areas will probably be in force by the time you read this.

seen it. You couldn't miss it. Planes are advised and any necessary course adjustments are made.

But if two planes *did* come within five miles of each other, an alarm would go off (a loud alarm), the situation would be immediately corrected—and the controller would be decertified on the spot. To the computer, and to the controller's bosses, a separation of 4.9 miles is the same as a collision.

Up until very recently, air controllers used to "eyeball" this separation, an amazing feat if you consider those tiny boxes and the tiny distances that separate them on a computer screen. Now an electronic circle appears around each box, graphically displaying the surrounding five miles. So now each plane travels in the equivalent of a five-mile bubble, and the edges of the bubbles are forbidden to touch.

You'll be reading more as we go along about the intricate national air traffic control system, historically reliable to an astonishing degree of accuracy but highly controversial in recent years. For now, let's worry about running into the ground.

Or some other feature of the landscape. The accident investigators have a name for this kind of crash, they call it "controlled flight into terrain." In other words, flying a perfectly functioning airplane into the ground (or water) with no prior awareness by the crew of any danger. And it used to happen disturbingly often. Between 1965 and 1975, a crash like that occurred six times a year, on average; seventeen times in the United States between 1971 and 1975. But in 1976, the first year a new device called the Ground Proximity Warning System (GPWS) was universally required in U.S. passenger aircraft (and in about 80 percent of commercial airliners worldwide), no such accidents occurred.[1] Since then, the single fatal airline incident under similar circumstances in this country was in 1978, when the GPWS sounded accurately, but was apparently turned off under very unusual conditions, and the plane came to rest in Escambia Bay, near Pensacola, Florida, resulting in the drowning deaths of three of the fifty-eight aboard.

The GPWS matches height data about the surrounding terrain with the plane's rate of descent. If the plane is closing too rapidly with the ground or water, an alarm goes off and a computer voice is activated: "PULL UP! PULL UP!" This onboard device has a counterpart in the system on the ground. The Minimum Safe Altitude Warning system

(MSAW) alerts the controller of unplanned descents to possibly dangerous levels. LOW ALT is flashed conspicuously on his screen.

Both of these systems were among several important changes instituted after a tragic 1974 accident outside Washington, D.C., when TWA
Flight 514 flew into Mount Weather a few miles from Dulles International Airport. Both are examples of systems to "back up" the humans
who are navigating planes, interpreting charts, directing planes from
the ground, or designing airports, for that matter. Which brings us to
the next common fear: fear of people.

The pilot is drunk or incompetent.

Legends of drunken airline pilots rank right up there with tales of
The Hook and ghostly hitchhikers and deaths foreshadowed in dreams
the night before the phone call came. Everyone has heard such a story,
and the tellers always swear it's based on personal experience—a pilot
they saw stumble out of a party on his way to the airport, an alcoholic
pilot that frequents *their brother-in-law's* bar. At least everyone likes to
tell *me* stories like that, maybe they just like what it does to the color of
my face. Nowadays, drug use is a popular variation.

In 1984, the National Transportation Safety Board released a study
on alcohol-related aviation accidents.[2] They found that about 10 percent of the *general* aviation accidents (private, business, and other non-
carrier planes) from 1975–81 had involved pilots under the influence of
alcohol. They also found this:

"No pilot of a U.S. certificated air carrier operated under 14 CFR
121 was found to have a positive alcohol test since at least 1964."

Part 14 CFR 121 is the part of the federal air regulations governing
large U.S. airlines (as opposed, for instance, to Part 135, which governs
commuters and air taxis). These are the most stringent laws on the
aviation books. The rules about drinking are not just pro forma or easy
to get around. No crew member can have a drink within eight hours of
a flight (those are the federal regulations; most airlines are much
stricter). A violation would just about end a pilot's professional career,
over and above an immediate suspension of his license to fly. But the

crews who fly with pilots are also deeply concerned about the possibility of his career and theirs being ended another way, like for instance in pieces on the ground. So the FAA is not the only party policing what would be a very dangerous situation—the airlines and the crews are vigilant, too. Whatever pilots do on their own time, the problem of alcohol's influence *in the cockpit* of major airlines has been virtually nonexistent.

As a matter of fact, most airlines have stringent rules even about prescription drugs, and even to the point of forbidding two members of the cockpit crew from eating the same meal immediately before or during a flight.

You'd call the FAA if you really *did* see a drunken pilot stumbling out of your brother-in-law's bar, wouldn't you? Boy, I would, in a heartbeat.

Incompetent pilots are harder to spot. How do *we* know what an incompetent pilot looks like? We've probably never seen one. There is an old saying among pilots, to the effect that doctors bury their mistakes but pilots are buried with theirs.

They may be hard for *us* to spot, but the FAA is not going by their looks. Nor are the airlines. Or the other pilots. There is another old saying: the pilot is always the first to arrive at the scene of an accident. If the guy sitting right next to you in the cockpit doesn't know what he's doing, you're going to arrive just about when he does.

A pilot is always on probation. Every six months, if he does not pass the exhaustive FAA physical, he's out of a job. Every year, if he doesn't pass all *three* of his annual performance tests (an in-flight "line" check, to examine his routine flying, and two "proficiency checks," during which he will have to perform satisfactorily on a series of devilishly contrived simulated emergencies), he's out of a job, either temporarily, if his errors weren't too bad and could be corrected by a lengthy period of retraining, or permanently. It's certainly not unheard of for a major airline pilot to flunk one of these tests. The whole objective is to make the tests hard enough to really examine performance. But I understand it's an acute professional embarrassment, enough so that one or two in an entire career is considered plenty. And during the year, if a pilot fails to perform on any of a number of other unannounced check rides, by the FAA or by other pilots in his own airline who are FAA-approved as examiners, he is, once again, out of the privilege to operate airplanes.

A pilot could be grounded, in fact, for a short time or forever, in many other ways. The captain of an airliner is held ultimately legally responsible for every aspect of the flight. No matter if he received bad information or followed a procedure which wasn't written correctly, no matter if he was acting in good faith on instructions from his company or from an air traffic controller or from anybody else, if something goes wrong and a plane under his command is involved in any infraction or incident whatsoever, he's liable to find himself suspended, guilty until proven innocent.

So you can be reasonably sure that if your pilot shows up at all, he has been making the right decisions and proving his ability to do so for a long time.

And, in general, you can make a few other assumptions by his presence in command of a passenger jet on a major airline. He is a specialist in the model you are flying. To change to another type he would have to undergo a complete additional course of tests and training in order to be "type rated" for that particular plane. He had to have a minimum of 1,500 flight hours to legally qualify for his present position, but the average pilot hired by a major airline in 1985 had over twice that many (3,832). That's new hires. By the time a pilot makes captain at a large airline, a process which still takes an average of eight to fourteen years, he will probably have flown about 10,000 hours with that airline alone.[3]

And he's "of good moral character" (well, that's what the regulations say; I'd like to be along on one of *those* check rides).

Before the airline industry was deregulated in 1978, leading to a sudden profusion in the number of airlines operating in this country, a person writing about airline pilot experience could have felt quite confident generalizing about *all* airlines and *all* airline pilots. Prior to deregulation, there were relatively few established airlines, and they have traditionally had roughly the same attitude toward the federal legal minimums (in everything, not just in pilot experience) that Diana of Wales has toward owning just enough clothes to stay warm. Now the major airlines are in white-hot competition with carriers that may, in some cases, be less able to afford such extravagance. Thus deregulation has become not just a political issue but a question of maintaining the extraordinarily high margins that have always been built around every aspect of American commercial aviation safety.

Flying big jets for big airlines is still pretty much the professional pinnacle for commercial pilots, so major airlines can still generally afford to be extremely picky about experience and other qualifications in the first place; and a newly hired pilot, his extensive previous military or commercial experience notwithstanding, can still expect to spend closely watched years working from flight engineer to copilot and eventually to captain.

But, to be fair, it's just as true that the youngest, most junior member of a cockpit crew for the newest airline must pass all the same annual tests—and then some, probably, if the FAA has any reason to suspect that standards are slipping at his operation. He is on the same continuing stringent probation to keep his job.

I'm sure airline deregulation has many fans among politicians and economists and airline executives and even among normal people, for all I know, but for those of us who were never that crazy about flying in the first place, the spectacle of airlines going in and out of business every time we turn around isn't exactly comforting. In almost every news story about commercial aviation we find some mention of deregulation, often portrayed as a dark force threatening to pull the entire system apart at the seams. And one of the worries at the top of our list is how our pilots are holding up.

We like to think of airline pilots as strong, silent, square-jawed, silvery haired, and imperturbable, sort of like the Lone Ranger, only more experienced. Now we see them on picket lines, not in the least silent, and a lot of them, especially on smaller airlines, don't seem all that silvery haired, either. How about the pilot in 1986 who, after a lengthy runway delay, turned his plane around, went back to the gate, parked, announced to his startled passengers that he was FED UP with delays, and walked off the plane? When you read about that, did you, for one brief sinking moment, think, "I knew it, the pilots are all finally cracking up"?

In general, the fear that deregulation would have a disastrous effect on safety has not been borne out by the facts. If anything, the safety record has gotten better: in the United States the eight years since 1978 have been the safest in history. For regional airlines, some of whom are the "upstart" operations of most concern to safety analysts, 1985 was the safest year ever. They have increased flight operations by 138 percent, and the number of accidents has declined from sixty-one in 1978 to seventeen in 1986.

It's certainly true that pilots, and other employees, at some airlines are up in arms about mergers, bankruptcies, pay and personnel cuts, and all the other ills the post-deregulation industry is heir to. During particularly heated negotiations, neither side—management or labor— seems to be above making a few veiled suggestions every once in a while that their adversaries across the bargaining table are toying with passenger safety. As a passenger, this is not the sort of thing I like to read in my morning newspaper. Now, granted, I've talked mostly to pilots about this, because frankly I don't much care what kind of mood the president of the airline is in while I'm flying, but I do like to see the pilot cheerful. I can only pass along the two facts that make *me* feel better.

One, the FAA keeps careful tabs on the financial status of airlines, and if a company is having trouble, or making major changes, such as merging, buying, or selling, it goes to the top of the list for inspections, surveillance, pilot checks, and overall intense scrutiny.

And two, a pilot may be protesting vociferously on the ground, but once he gets onboard a plane his interest is identical to yours. No one is more intimately concerned with the safety of an airline than the pilot who has to get on a company plane every day of his working life. A pilot who isn't convinced he can complete a flight with safety, for whatever reason, won't take off (even if the reason is that runway delays have put him in an extremely bad mood). I realize his‡ concern is mostly selfish. As long as pilots stay selfish, I don't mind if they get less silvery haired.

---

‡ I know I mentioned this previously, but all the "he's" are making me nervous. I must remind you again that there are an increasing number of "she's" in the nation's cockpits, and they have to undergo the same rigorous training and continuing proof of their abilities as their male counterparts.

The weather is too bad for flying.

Modern technology has steadily decreased the fraction of weather that represents a danger to airline flight. The automatic takeoff and landing systems on big jets don't need to be able to "see" the runway; radio beams guide the plane down a precise unerring track (although a pilot still needs to see more of the runway during landing than during takeoff, which is why the weather a thousand miles away at your destination can delay your flight even when conditions where you're taking off wouldn't).

Altitudes above 30,000 feet or so, where airliners generally cruise, are also above most of the clouds, strong winds, ice, and other messy weather lower-flying small planes have to contend with.

Sophisticated radar systems onboard and at the air traffic control centers can spot most hazardous weather—categorize it very precisely, in fact—and direct flights around it. Before each flight, the pilot has studied weather forecasts for the enroute phase, the destination airport, and alternate airports.

Both preflight and enroute, continuous access to detailed descriptions of temperatures, cloud types and measurements, winds, fronts, storms, jet streams, and other meteorological items makes it possible to plan flights which avoid not only most serious weather difficulties, but even most *bumpy* areas that might give the customers an uncomfortable ride.

You notice I keep saying "most." Let's get right to the heart of this fear, shall we? You're not afraid of "most" bad weather, a little rain, a little wind, a little fog. The National Oceanic and Atmospheric Administration has been flying assorted airplanes directly through hurricanes (250 m.p.h. winds is the record to date) and intense thunderstorms since 1956, and they haven't lost one yet. Not that a passenger jet would be anybody's first choice for a hurricane research plane, but you get the idea your battleship-strength craft isn't going to be bothered by much. You're probably prepared to be tolerant when your plane hits some unexpected turbulence, because you know from planning picnics on the advice of TV weathermen that forecasting is an inexact science.

No, you're talking about BAD weather. Blizzards, thunderstorms.

And if you've read a newspaper in the last five years, you're probably talking about wind shear.

Blizzards can be forecast, and the airports, airlines, and air traffic control system can gear up the runways and planes for them. If conditions fall below prescribed minimums, flights are cancelled, but in general snowstorms are low-level weather systems, so once the plane gets safely off, the problem is pretty much over. I see hands going up all over the room, and I know you want to remind me of the 1982 Air Florida accident in Washington, D.C., which none of us is likely to forget, but, as you will see later on, much more than the weather went wrong on that terrible day. Snow can be dealt with effectively. The performance of a specific model of jetliner in such conditions has been explicitly analyzed and the safe ranges are well understood by experienced pilots. Deicing technology and procedures are sophisticated. I'm told jet travel in Minnesota is quite common.

Thunderstorms, in themselves, are not the problem. If planes couldn't fly safely through thunderstorms, most of the air service to most of the nation would be shut down every summer. Wind shears, in themselves, are not the problem. If you have flown a great deal, you may even have flown through a wind shear—a sudden dramatic change in the wind's speed and direction—once or twice in your time. It may have rattled the trays, may even have temporarily shifted your stomach to your mouth for a few seconds, but it didn't really threaten your plane (although you may be sure it got the attention of your pilot). Flights are studiously planned and flown to avoid thunderstorms and wind shears, if at all possible, partly to allow for smoother, less exciting flights.

But mostly to avoid the merest possibility of a certain kind of thunderstorm, which may give rise to a certain kind of wind shear, which *is* the problem: a microburst.[4]

You'd probably be wasting your energy to worry about flying in any other kind of "bad" weather. But I can understand being scared of microbursts, because a microburst is one terrifying little memmajemma. It can only seriously threaten your plane under very specific conditions, however, so let me tell you about them so you won't mistakenly worry *every minute*.

The most powerful microburst recorded—more than twice as powerful as the one that caused the 1985 Delta crash in Dallas—occurred at

Andrews Air Force Base, near Washington, D.C., on August 1, 1983, smack-dab on the runway, six minutes after the landing of Air Force One carrying the President of the United States. Never has Mr. Reagan's well-known luck been more dramatically demonstrated.

A microburst is a sudden, immensely powerful downdraft. As it hits the ground with explosive force, it spreads out in a curling vortex. Microbursts reduce buildings to splinters every once in a while, but you probably don't read about that because you're too busy poring over the paper looking for bad airplane news.

Microbursts develop and dissipate rapidly, over a period of about five to fifteen minutes, maybe two to four minutes at their most severe, and they affect a small area, a mile or so, on average. So they are difficult to predict, to detect, and to deal with *if* a plane is already very close to the ground, during the first minutes of takeoff or the last few minutes of landing. Two of the most catastrophic recent airliner crashes—the 1982 Pan Am accident in New Orleans and the 1985 Dallas tragedy—and since 1964 perhaps twenty-seven other accidents or incidents worldwide, the majority nonfatal, involved microbursts or freakishly severe wind shears. Some past accidents which seemed inexplicable at the time are also being reevaluated in light of current knowledge about microbursts.

You may rest assured that, as rare as the threat is, the FAA, the airlines, the pilots, and the weather research community are no more nonchalant about this frightening phenomenon than we are. To give you just one example of the intense level of concern, the FAA has awarded a large contract to a team including Boeing, Lockheed, Douglas, United Airlines, and the U. S. National Center for Atmospheric Research to develop a state-of-the-art package for pilot training in microburst avoidance and reaction techniques. Meanwhile, pilots practice flying through microbursts in simulators as part of their ongoing training, and researchers continue to identify more precisely the characteristic conditions which can give rise to microbursts, and thus to give pilots increasingly well-defined clues about what to look for and avoid.

So if your flight is delayed, you might spend a little of the waiting time writing the pilot a thank-you note. About 65 percent of delays are caused by the weather. But in the twenty years between 1961 and 1981, weather was the major cause factor in only about 5 percent of catastrophic accidents worldwide, so I'd say the waiting around paid off handsomely.[5] You should probably not be nervous about taking off if the people making the decisions aren't nervous enough to prevent you.

Maybe one in every 100–200 thunderstorms will develop a microburst. But remember this: to cause trouble for the exact plane you're on, a microburst would have to materialize at the exact wrong place on the exact wrong runway, at the exact wrong instant at the exact most vulnerable point in your plane's takeoff or landing. If you want to keep this particular fear, I won't try to argue you out of it, but you should plan to worry only during the first five and the last five minutes of your flight, *if* there's a raging thunderstorm going on. If you're a Republican, I wouldn't even worry then.

Something will happen during turbulence. (The plane will flip over or break or fall or SOMETHING.)

You mustn't say there is "nothing" between you and the ground when you're in an airplane, because that would be unreasonably insulting the air, and you don't want to do that because the air is holding you up. An ocean of air. This is not just some poetic metaphor I composed to cheer you up, it's quite literally so. But if you're on a boat, and it bobs in the current, I bet you don't think you're immediately going to dive to the bottom of the sea, unless you are an aquaphobe, in which case you're reading the wrong book. Turbulence in the air has its counterparts in white water on a stream, or foam on waves, or ripples on a pond.

Airliners even leave wakes, just like boats. Pilots make every effort to avoid these wakes, not because they're particularly dangerous to a large airliner in flight (although they can be very dangerous for a small plane), but because they make a big pronounced bump. I hit one once. The pilot came on the intercom and politely apologized, but I looked around at my fellow passengers and concluded that he and I were the only people on the plane who had noticed—or would *admit* it, anyway.

Turbulence does not seriously disturb the plane's flight because, as you saw previously, planes are fundamentally designed to stabilize themselves. Air may push the plane down, but it pops back up like a cork. Not only are all the gadgets on your *empennage* reacting continuously to the motion of the air, but the automatic pilots on sophisticated passenger jets make constant, subtle corrections. Autopilots respond to changes in air movement, and to the always changing balance of the plane as fuel is used and people wander around the cabin. They make these adjustments with a speed and delicacy your human pilot would have a hard time duplicating. There's even a special "turb-mode" for autopilots, to put this compensating effect into high gear.

When the weather outside your plane is lousy, you might have *yourself* on turb-mode, but if you're flying on a nice clear day and hit some turbulence you may take the surprise as a personal affront. What has probably happened is a few swipes from the paw of CAT (Clear Air Turbulence). CAT is usually associated with the jet streams, fast-flowing rivers of air set up by the rotation of the earth. Where the jet streams are on a given day is reasonably subject to forecast. If you're flying west to east, it would be nice if you could get directly into one. The strong tailwind would speed your flight up considerably. But right on the *edge* of a jet stream is a particularly turbulent place to be, and air currents being their normal fluid unpredictable selves, CAT can sometimes sneak up on a plane. "Air pocket" is a bit of a misnomer, since it implies an empty space, of which there are none in the sky until you get farther out in space than airliners fly. The whole place is chock-full of air molecules that look like nothing to you but mean a great deal to an airplane. CAT, however, can make you *feel* as if you've dropped into a little sky pocket.

The last thing you should worry about is your *plane*. To meet the federal rules, big planes must be able to fly undisturbed when assaulted by at least 2 g's (twice their loaded weight) of force.[6] But as you may be noticing, manufacturers are an obsessive-compulsive lot. The Boeing engineer I asked about this actually sounded *insulted* when I mentioned the 2 g rule. Modern airliners can withstand upward of 6–7 g's, and do so routinely during their testing.* As a point of reference, turbulence of .4 g's, repeat *point*-4, is characterized as "severe." During part of one of the tests for any airliner, machines called "flutter" boxes are attached to its wings, to simulate *extreme* turbulence (which is one step up from

---

* The various formulae for airliner certification are dauntingly complex; if you're interested in a little more explanation, please check the Notes section.

"severe"). So the test pilots fly around for a while with the plane being shaken so hard they can't read the instruments. This is their idea of a day at the office. Your plane will be fine.

If you have to worry, worry about *yourself.* There have certainly been turbulence-related injuries, most of the serious ones to flight attendants who were up and about in the course of their duties. But very few (one study of the 1977–85 period found *none)* have happened to a passenger who was *wearing a properly fastened seat belt.* [7] Pay attention to the seat belt sign, to take care of the turbulence the pilot knows about, and keep your seat belt fastened while you're in your seat, to take care of any turbulence he finds out about the same time you do. The Air Line Pilots Association worked for twelve years to get those little tags on every seat telling people to keep their seat belts fastened. If you pay attention, you should be able to fly almost as serenely through turbulence as your plane can.

Incidentally, nobody says you have to *like* that funny, falling, air pocket feeling, although apparently roller coasters were invented for people who love it. Even newborn infants will exhibit the "startle response" if they feel themselves falling, and anybody over six years old has learned to associate sudden weightlessness with the uncontrolled-contact-with-playground-terrain that usually follows. I *hate* that feeling, and you probably do, too, and I will defend our right to say "Yipes" if we hit an air pocket, no matter how fearless about flying we may become.

But for run-of-the-mill choppy air, try to remember you're on the functional equivalent of a very big, very fast, very expensive motorboat.

The engines will stop suddenly in midair.

All right, I'll admit it. This was my personal all-time worst fear. Maybe it's because I used to have a 1972 Camaro whose engine would do precisely that, a couple of times a week—be humming along the freeway in fine Camaro style and then suddenly just cease upon the night. [8] I figured someday sooner or later I'd be cruising along in the heavens and my plane's engines would do the same thing.

I was once sitting in a plane, getting ready to take off, quietly preparing to meet my Maker, and just as we had taxied to the point where we would begin our takeoff run, the pilot announced that we were going to have to turn around, go back to the gate, and restart one of our engines with "external power."

I could not believe my ears. The pilot was quite openly admitting to me that the plane I was on had to be *jump-started*. If you can't get the engines to start, doesn't that mean there's something wrong with them? Doesn't that mean that we are getting ready to fly from Washington to Kansas City in a plane with *broken engines?* I was so flabbergasted I ended up having a fairly peaceful flight. It was like flying in a catatonic trance.

So you see I took quite a lively interest in checking up on jet engines.

First, an airliner has at least two—DC-10s and L-1011s have three, 747s have four—each operating, as you know, on entirely independent systems. So for, say, three of them to conk out simultaneously in flight is sort of analogous to my Camaro's engine choosing to quit at the same moment as the engines of two of the cars passing me in the next lane.

That is, the situation would be similar except that jet engines are maintained with considerably more zeal and expertise than my Camaro engine was. And even if the two cars passing me are maintained better, they are still not as reliable, by their very design, as a jet engine. Automobile engines, as all airplane engines used to be, are piston engines: lots of parts moving up and down, lots of sparking and timing involved to keep the thing going. In jet engines, all the parts are going in one direction. A turbojet is like a barrel with both ends open. Great quantities of air are sucked into the front end and compressed. In the center of the barrel is a combustion chamber, where the compressed air and a constant spray of fuel are mixed. As the mixture burns, its temperature and pressure rise sharply. It expands by rushing out the back of the barrel. As long as there's air, as long as there's fuel, all the blades do is spin. And according to Newton's Third Law of Motion, for every action there is an equal and opposite reaction. The hot gases rush rearward and the plane rushes equally and oppositely forward.

Engines are torture-tested, just like airplanes. The manufacturers shoot water, ice slabs, hail, and frozen chickens into the test models. I think the airline industry must use as much dead poultry as Colonel Sanders. For example, the FAA requires that an engine be able to simultaneously ingest eight one-and-a-half-pound birds without losing more than 25 percent thrust.

In photographs taken immediately after a 1975 crash caused by a microburst at Denver's Stapleton airport (luckily, no one was killed, but the plane was destroyed), you can plainly see the dust being kicked up around the broken plane. The engines were still running.

Now, of course, even jet engines are not perpetual motion machines. An airliner engine is shut down in flight for some reason or another about once every ten thousand flights or so. In the majority of such instances, the engine has not been "lost," in the sense that it is suddenly completely useless, but instead the pilots have turned it off deliberately because they have noticed indications that it's not working properly and they don't want to run it until it's *really* damaged.

Because *one* airliner engine costs from $3–4 million. If you've ever driven a car for any distance after the oil light came on, your mechanic's bill was probably only about half that, but now that you know how much jet engines cost, you know why the airlines make such an effort to maintain and operate them to precise standards. It isn't *just* because they know how upset we would get if an engine on our flight had to be shut down.

You can get where you're going safely, albeit much more slowly, on one engine (a 747 would pretty much need two), and all jets are certified so that if they blew an engine precisely during takeoff, the most critical point, they could still get safely into (and out of) the air.

In fact, all weights and fuel loads for every flight are predicated on the loss of one engine. But even though you could continue the flight with an engine turned off, airliners aren't allowed to. By law, failure of an engine for any reason is an automatic emergency requiring the pilot to turn back, or land at the nearest airport. The general rule is that two-engine passenger planes can be no farther than sixty miles from an airport at any point in their flight. Three- or four-engine planes, no farther than two hours' flying time on one engine. Flights that cross the ocean are planned so that the flight could continue safely to its destination even if two of its engines failed in the exact middle of the ocean (in the twenty-odd years they have been flying, *no* passenger jet has ever had to ditch in the middle of the ocean—don't put off that trip to Hawaii another day). The only exception to date to the ocean-crossing rule is now pending for the two-engine 767, which has had to meet especially stringent tests for backup systems. It's taken about thirty years for the FAA to become sufficiently convinced of the jet engine's reliability to consider making such an exception.

Just as an example of that reliability, the Pratt & Whitney JT8D series of engines are the most widely used in commercial aviation, powering about two thirds of the U.S. fleet and about 95 percent of the non-Communist world's, not counting jumbo jets. The first version of the JT8D was introduced in 1964, and while it was new, before it had become anywhere near as widespread as now, a JT8D engine used to be shut down an average of once in every two years of service.[9]

There are now over twelve thousand such engines worldwide. The current average in-flight shutdown rate—a measure of how often the pilot has to shut down the engine for *any* reason, whether it could remain functional or not—is once every *thirteen* years.

But what *if* all the engines somehow went kerflooey and had to be shut down during flight? Ah, now you are not talking about fear of engine failure. Now you are showing signs of being afraid that:

The plane will suddenly go into a nosedive and fall out of the sky like a wounded duck.

This is the real reason you and I and so many fearful fliers are so worried about the engines. And this is the core fear for those who are not nearly as afraid of dying as they are of *falling*.

Even if a plane was suddenly deprived of *all* engine power, it would not plummet like a rock. The engines are not holding the plane up. Gliders don't have any engines at all. They have to be towed up *into* the sky, but they fly just fine once they're there. Well, your plane is a glider, too. Literally. The multimillion-dollar investment in mighty engines is primarily to allow for speedy forward progress, the reason most business travelers choose jets over gliders.

You remember lift and drag. All planes have a certain "lift-to-drag" ratio, depending on their design. A 747, for instance, has a lift-to-drag ratio of about seventeen which means that, *without power*, for every foot it descends, it glides forward at least seventeen feet. On a slight slope of about three degrees. The design engineers and computer experts are not the only ones vouching for this; test pilots turn off all the engines to test it. As the plane descends, the increased airspeed over the wings intensifies the good old Bernoulli effect, thus increasing lift.

We also have another one of Newton's laws of motion on our side here, this time the First Law, which states that once a body is in motion it tends to stay in motion unless acted upon by an outside force. Once a plane has reached cruising altitude and cruising speed, it is a body in motion and tends to remain in motion at that speed. Actually, the heavier a plane is, the more stubbornly it tends to stay in motion. Believe it or not, a pilot will start slowing down a heavily loaded jumbo jet for landing long before he would have to start with a lighter plane, because the heavier jet is, simply stated, harder to stop flying.

"Oh, sure," I can hear you saying, "Newton, Schmewton, that's just *theoretical.*" So here is an example from life.

In this example, the precise kind of weird, all-but-impossible mix-up so dear to the imaginations of fearful fliers everywhere actually occurred, in 1983, and just about *everything* went wrong at once: human errors, a maintenance foul-up, fuel exhaustion, resulting engine failure, you name it. A Canadian 767 took off from Montreal with roughly half the fuel the crew *thought* it was taking off with. As usual with airplane problems, the links in this chain of events were many and unlikely, but what the problem boiled down to was several people (first at Montreal, and then *again* at Ottawa on the next stop) accidentally conspiring to miscalculate between centimeters and liters and kilograms and pounds in a situation where they wouldn't have had to do any hand-calculating in the first place if the fuel gauge had been fixed. And it came to pass that at 37,000 feet, this perfectly good plane, through no fault of its own, ran out of gas. This did not, of course, bother the plane too much. It kept on doing what planes do, which is fly, but the crew did not take this surprise so lightly. I guess they decided maybe they'd better land before anything *else* went wrong.

The best landing spot, they determined, was an old, now-abandoned airstrip, and so they glided in. The place was abandoned as an *airstrip,* but it had been turned into a drag racing strip, and today, as it happened, was Race Day. The last scheduled event had just concluded, but the spectators milling around the stands were treated to the added attraction of an airliner settling silently out of the sky and sliding to a stop right in front of their eyes ("Dang, Bobby, this is even better than the tractor pull last week!"). Everyone was real surprised. The passengers emerged, a few with minor injuries, and all, I am guessing, strongly resolved to stop and smell the roses.[10]

Now, I'm not suggesting you should expect this much excitement on your next plane ride, or at your next drag race, either (you may want to stick around after the last race, just in case). And about as many circumstances went exactly right on that day as went exactly wrong. All I am suggesting is that many of us have an unfounded suspicion that the plane *wants* to plunge out of the sky and only the most strenuous maneuvers keep it flying, and any little thing might screw up the entire magic. The pilot is *not* constantly wrestling the controls in a heroic struggle to defy gravity. A plane needs some persuading to get into the sky, and to stop flying, but not to fly.

Incidentally, as delighted as I was to find out that airliners are efficient gliders if they have to be, you should have known your neurotic-on-the-spot would not rest until she had satisfied herself that this gliding thing doesn't happen *all the time*. I like fun as much as the next person, but I had some train schedules I wanted to check if the occasion for a powerless glide comes up very often. I knew it was rare. Everyone kept telling me, "It's rare, it's very, very rare." I have, quite frankly, driven my sources crazy on this point.

I have found three incidents in the United States since 1980 through the first half of 1986 where at some point during the flight all the engines were turned off and pilots had to glide the planes for a brief period before restarting one or more in order to land—on an Eastern L-1011, a United 767, and a Republic DC-9—all in 1983. The reasons for each were very different and very unusual, but careful investigations and new preventive measures followed, just the same. Each of these planes landed without further incident. No one aboard was injured, although I suspect they considered the developments quite incident enough for one day.

I know. This makes 1983 sound like Year of the Aerial Camaro. I really sort of debated whether or not I should even *tell* you about these weird occurrences, but every time I considered just saying, "Oh, this kind of thing never happens, trust me," I felt my nose getting ready to

sprout. Still, it's worth keeping in mind that just from 1980 through
1985 more than 30 million airline flights took off and landed (sans
gliding) in the United States. Three is a number like Monday, Tuesday,
Wednesday. Thirty million is a number like how many days there are in
roughly eighty-two thousand years. So I guess that qualifies glides as
very, very rare.

If I had been on one of those three planes, I'd probably just now be
regaining the use of speech, but, on balance, I still say a glide is better
than a nosedive—of which, I can say with no fear of nose-lengthening,
there have not been any.

The emergency door will fly open and suck you out.

I know it can feel a little dicey sitting right next to the emergency
door. Doors open, right? And if *this* one opens, there isn't anything
between you and a very high dive. They never look all that secure to
me, either. "Don't open in flight" doesn't sound like a particularly
severe warning. Actually, though, emergency doors *can't* open in flight.
They are designed to be just the slightest bit bigger than the opening. In
flight, the pressure inside the plane is higher than the pressure outside,
so the doors are being pressed against an opening too small for them.
That's why they call them "plug"-type doors.

In the past year or so I've found a couple of cases of very strange
passengers *trying* to open emergency doors in flight. It's never been
quite clear to me, or possibly to them, why. The latest one was on an
airliner beginning its final descent into Philadelphia. The young man
was arrested and charged with the federal crime of interfering with and
assaulting a flight crew, and he discovered, as others of his persuasion
have before him, that the harder you push against an emergency door,
the tighter the seal becomes.

Even allowing for the fact that you might be in the way of some
people with fascinating psychological profiles, right next to an emergency door is an extremely safe place to sit, because you *could* open it
on the ground, which is the only place you might need it.

Lightning will strike the plane.

Lightning does strike planes quite often. You probably haven't noticed because a plane is designed to shed lightning the way a duck sheds water. If you knew what to look for, and were allowed on the runway, and had nothing better to do, you could probably see the little discolorations and pocks on an airliner where lightning had glanced off. If lightning strikes the nose or some other large part of the plane, it is conducted off harmlessly to the ground. If it strikes a smaller part, like the wingtip, it may make a tiny hole, about the size of a dime. You probably wouldn't even hear the bang, because a plane traveling 500 m.p.h. will have moved a considerable distance before the sound really registers. A lightning bolt struck a Piedmont jet as it was coming up to the gate after landing at D.C.'s National Airport in September 1984. No one on the plane was hurt at all. Several ground personnel were taken to the hospital for observation but released almost immediately. They were described as "shook-up." I'll bet.

There was a terrible accident in 1963 where lightning was suspected. The apparent scenario was that, through a freak occurrence, a bolt of lightning had struck the exact point on the wing where fuel fumes were being exhausted, and the resulting explosion destroyed the plane. Now, you might think that the airlines would be justified in thinking that, even if the conjectured sequence was indeed correct, it was due to an unbelievably unlikely event, with a literally one-in-billions chance of reoccurring. This perhaps understandable position was not taken. It's hardly ever taken in the aviation business. Instead, the entire fuel exhausting systems of *all* passenger planes were redesigned, and even that tiny vulnerable element corrected. Since then there have been no similar incidents.† In all probability, the freak occurrence just hasn't been repeated, but if it has, the change has saved many lives.

† An Iranian 747 on a military mission exploded in 1976 under suspicious circumstances, and a lightning strike was considered a possibility, assuming the plane hadn't been modified (it wasn't a passenger carrier), but sabotage and a number of other factors were also investigated.

The plane will run out of gas, or the wrong kind of gas will be put in.

The wrong kind of gas isn't much of a problem, since all jets run on the same kind of fuel—Jet A—and so that's the only kind of fuel likely to be in the airport's fuel trucks. Jet fuel is not like comparatively explosive gasoline, but more like heating oil, which burns slowly at a steadier, predictable rate. Putting jet fuel into a small plane is a hazard, though, and so a system of color-coding the ground fuel system and the airplane's fuel equipment has been established for them.

I think the fear of running *out* of gas is sort of a holdover from our familiar tendency as drivers to say, "Hmmm, I'm on E, let's see how much farther I can go." Still, you already know about one case of fuel exhaustion in an airliner, and there have been a few others.

The reason these cases are so extremely rare is because fuel is checked so often, by so many people, before a plane takes off, and substantial reserves are calculated for a range of alternative possibilities in flight—bad weather at the destination airport, for instance. The plane must carry at least enough fuel to get to the scheduled airport, go from there to an alternate, and, once there, cruise for an additional forty-five minutes. The airline's flight dispatcher indicates fuel requirements on the flight plan which the pilot receives and checks and approves pre-flight, the pilot makes his own calculations and the final decision, the airline ground personnel are checking the fuel being loaded, and then the crew checks the fuel all over again once they're onboard.

The procedures before takeoff are not a casual product of whatever the captain feels like doing that particular day. They are spelled out precisely. To give you an idea, federal regulations require that cockpit checklists must be carried covering at least the following situations: steps before starting engines, before takeoff, during cruise, before landing, after landing, stopping engines, emergencies, and climb performance data. But no major airliner in the United States takes off with just *that* meager amount of paperwork. The cockpit on your flight is a mini-reference library of manuals, advisories, reporting forms, charts, maintenance logs, and—checklists. And on all the preflight checklists, fuel loads figure prominently. And on all the enroute checklists, steps for *monitoring* fuel use rates.

In the hypercompetitive atmosphere since deregulation, airlines have become very interested in fuel efficiency. Partly for that reason, and partly to reduce stresses on the air traffic control system, far fewer fuel-guzzling holding patterns are created today than even a few years ago. Safety is a factor, too. Unusually lengthy holding patterns figured in more than one serious accident in the past. If flights have to do any waiting around, the pilots and the controllers prefer that they do it on the ground. Before 1981, the year of the infamous air traffic controllers' strike, about 55 percent of all aircraft delayed were held in the air. Currently, only about 10 percent are.[11]

A wing will fall off.

I can't vouch for every single model of airplane in the sky, but if you are riding on a Boeing 727, 737, 747, 757, 767, a DC-8, DC-9, DC-10, a Lockheed L-1011, or an Airbus A-300 or A-310, and a wing falls off, you might take some small comfort in the fact that you are making aviation history because it has NEVER happened before.

I mention those models specifically because they make up over 95 percent of the U.S. major airline fleet. If I wanted to list every model of airplane off of which a wing has never fallen, I could fill up the rest of the book.

The rules for airliner certification are that if any part or system affecting the plane's ability to fly can conceivably fail, that part or system has to be backed up by at least one, and usually more than one, part or system. If the part *can't* be backed up (planes wouldn't fly so well with four wings each), then the part *can't* fail. Period. The chances of the part failing for any reason must be exhaustively demonstrated to be no more than *one in a thousand million*.

A plane could theoretically fly missing some pretty big parts, all other conditions being favorable. There is a famous photograph of a B-52 flying coolly along without its tail. One of the engines on a 727 fell off in flight once *(once)*.[12] You can't see the engines of a 727 from the cockpit, but the pilot noticed a warning light indicating that one of the engines was "malfunctioning," so he turned it off and made plans to land. He thought he was turning it off. It was already about halfway to the ground by then. The flight attendant came forward to tell him one of the passengers was pretty sure an engine had fallen off. The pilot couldn't believe it. After the plane landed on schedule, the pilot took a look, and sure enough, he owed the flight attendant an apology. The plane, missing an engine, hadn't missed a beat.‡

But we need those wings. So the wings and the sections around them are the strongest structures on the plane.

For instance. A wing is designed to flex up and down in flight. I'm sure you've noticed this as you checked the wing for gremlins unscrewing the bolts. In an extremely bad storm, worse than you're likely to be flying in, a wing might flex as much as a foot. Well, in the manufacturer's torture chamber, the wing will be flexed until it breaks. Maybe, on average, about twenty feet. Each way. Which means that, if the wing were flapping like a bird's, it could safely describe an arc of at least forty feet. Then the engineers will take a hacksaw and cut through various parts of it, and once again, it will be flexed until it breaks.

The essential wing structures are built to be so strong that even in the few infrequent cases when a *piece* of a wing—a slat, for instance, or an outer panel—has fallen off an airliner in flight, the planes involved have landed safely.

Really, for your own self-respect, choose something else besides the wing falling off to be afraid of. You don't want to get like those people who are afraid of moths.

Something will happen in the toilet.

Many of those who take fear of flying seminars voice this fear. I guess if you're already feeling vulnerable, you feel really vulnerable in the toilet. I always ran *to* the toilet when I was afraid. I felt safer there than in my seat, and less inhibited about wailing aloud.

Actually, the toilet is not a dangerous place to be. You can't get sucked down the toilet. You are, even if you were born yesterday, too big. Actually, you may have noticed in a few planes that even the stuff

‡ I'd say this occurrence was pretty rare. Boeing estimates that a 727 is taking off somewhere in the world about once every four seconds.

that's supposed to get sucked down the toilet occasionally does not. And, anyway, the toilet isn't a direct route to sky. You would've heard a very big public outcry by now if it were.

The only thing you want to watch about the toilet is being there when the seat belt sign is turned on. Turbulence is more pronounced in the back of the plane. I've heard stories about people being—let's see— involved in romantic encounters in airline toilets. I even saw it in a movie once but I've been unable to figure out how they—well, anyway, whatever you're doing back there, if the seat belt sign goes on, finish up. You want to bump neither your head nor anything else.

Of course, I'm assuming that what you're doing back there does not involve smoking. Apart from the fact that smoking *anywhere* is several thousand times more dangerous than being on an airplane, about the last place a lighted cigarette should be is in an airplane lavatory. Serious in-flight fires are extremely rare (to date, the single recorded fatality on a U.S. carrier jet due to an in-flight fire was an apparent suicide), but deadly enough to warrant extreme caution. In June 1983, an Air Canada DC-9 landed at the Greater Cincinnati Airport with a raging fire aboard. Twenty-three passengers died of smoke and toxic fume inhalation; most of the twenty-three others who escaped had been able to breathe through moistened towels until the plane landed. The fire started in an aft lavatory, and even though the exact origin has never been established conclusively, a cigarette smoldering in the trash receptacle couldn't be ruled out. I know *you* would never dream of carrying anything lit into an airplane toilet, but if you see anybody else doing it, I'd suggest snitching on them in short order.

You will fall out of the plane.

This used to be a very funny fear. For years, I thought I was the only one who had it, and I kept it a deep secret, and tried to face up to the fact that if I, and I alone, were plucked out of a flying airliner, my number could not be any more up than that. I still kept a wary eye on the floor, vividly picturing it ripping asunder and all of us dropping out of the sky like toys out of a pinata.

I've found out since that many fearful fliers have this same deep secret fear. Again, I scoured the records. A stewardess fell out of a plane in the early sixties, before plug-type doors were universally used, and the door had been broken for some time. A man from Beaumont, Texas, fell out of a plane in 1973, under circumstances so bizarre that even the accident investigators were at a loss finally to explain how such a combination of things could have happened, but a number of changes were made nonetheless, just to make sure the consequences would never be the same, even if the bizarre sequence repeated itself. The plane landed safely and no one else was seriously injured.*[13]

The fact is, there are no ways to just "fall" out of a modern airliner. The doors don't open. The toilet's too small. The windows aren't operable and are built to bulge about eight inches before they'd break out. If you sawed a hole in the floor, you'd fall into the luggage compartment. The fuselage of a plane is so overdesigned for structural soundness that most of the floors and walls remain intact even after crashes.

But it is difficult to smile at this fear now. Just about the only element capable of overriding the obvious and otherwise unquestioned security of a passenger inside a plane is another human being's deliberate, malevolent intent to destroy. In April 1986, the deaths in Greece of four Americans were caused by such an intent. The plane landed safely with a gaping hole torn in its side, which I suppose is further proof of an airliner's general invulnerability, but most of us are feeling very vulnerable indeed, these days. Not just on planes, of course, and that is why I don't have much to say on the subject of terrorism. Security on airliners and in airports has been stepped up to unprecedented levels, in hopes that the success of previous similar efforts will be repeated (in 1980 there were twenty-one successful hijackings in the United States, down to two brief unsuccessful attempts in 1985 that ended without injury to anyone).[14] But the threat elsewhere—in public buildings, in front of hotels, in discothèques and streetside cafés—is just as real. I'm an American, living in a country where political movements spend millions of dollars to create wonderful images, so I can't explain any better than anybody else why entire nations would go out of their way to give their causes the most repugnant public relations in history.

I'll just go on with my little book, hoping that you and I will be able

* I'll try to explain this weird incident to you in the Notes, if you're really interested, but the circumstances really don't apply to planes flying now.

to separate fear of political, religious, and general madness from fear of flying.

I'll tell you one thing, though. I sure don't mind going through security. I've talked to some businessmen who were much more terrified by the thought of spending two or three hours being searched before every flight than they were of anything that could happen *on* the flight. But not me. Once in Dallas the authorities confiscated my scissors. I couldn't really picture myself hijacking a plane with a pair of scissors—pilots don't look to me like they could be intimidated by threats of snipping—but that's been the only contribution required of me so far in the effort to ensure safer skies, and I was glad to make it. I turned the scissors over without a squeak. And I'm quite prepared to do more, if more is required.

Entrusting Your Life to Strangers

Every flight, like every wedding, is a complex interaction of myriad groups and individuals, leading one to worry not *if* something will go wrong, but at which point in the network. Weddings, however, are not conducted with the same rigorous attention to detail as American commercial aviation, although you would not know it by reading *Bride* Magazine. Even if they were, weddings would still be terrifying.

The fact is that very few human endeavors are executed with as much compulsive *institutional* attention to detail as airline passenger flights. It is sort of a paradox that the main reason *we* do not need to be afraid of crashes is that a powerful, pervasive fear of crashes underlies the entire system, extending to virtually every person, procedure, regulation, and piece of equipment having anything at all to do with a passenger flight. The more I found out about how planes are built and maintained and operated, and about how every aspect of aviation safety is under constant, intense review by researchers and industry analysts all over the world, the sillier I felt about how I used to sit on flights and agonize about my safety.

I felt as if I'd gone to the Pentagon and said, "See here, fellows, it's a dangerous world out there, don't you think we should buy some guns or something?"

As an airline passenger, I'm depending on thousands of strangers, the majority of whom I will never see, not only the pilot and copilot and flight attendants, but test pilots, designers, manufacturers, mechanics, traffic controllers, flight managers, technicians, trainers, government personnel, investigators, inspectors, supervisors, inspectors of supervisors, et cetera, et cetera.

Almost every one of these strangers, of course, is much better qualified and more stringently checked up on than any of the other strangers to whom I entrust my life every day with hardly a thought. At least I don't *think* the guy who fixed my car's brakes had to pass a federal examination, followed by his company's initial and recurrent training courses, before he was allowed to use his federal license, which could be promptly lifted if one of the federal inspectors on his job premises almost daily (as they are at most big airline maintenance centers) noticed an irregular procedure.

But I don't want to spend my time before a flight researching the résumés and family histories of every person who ever touched my plane in a professional capacity, even assuming I could obtain that very long list, so what I care about is the *system*. And what I am looking for in particular is a system that prevents most mistakes, catches most of the rest early, and works to keep the consequences small when a mistake *does* get by.

I mean so small I do not notice it. I'm prepared to overlook a little mishandled luggage and a few untidy rest rooms, but if there are any problems with the way the plane is built or flown or controlled, I consider those the *system's* problems, and I expect them to be corrected long before they come to my attention, and never ONCE while I'm actually *using* the plane.

It may sound as if I'm asking a lot, but that is the kind of system that almost one million American commercial airline passengers every day have come to expect, and that is the way they expect it to work on every one of the roughly sixteen thousand flights they daily board. Most of them just take the system on faith, and travel as trusting as puppies. You don't have to.

Now, I should admit at the outset that this system we are talking about is far from flawless. I admit it so that you will know that I have not been living on Mars, which is where you would have to be stationed to avoid hearing regular installments of What's Wrong with Aviation

This Time. I won't try to discuss every air travel issue now current; during the normal shelf life of a book, the controversies-of-the-week are bound to change numerous times. I only want to say a few words in defense of bad publicity.

Yes, you heard me correctly. Yes, I know that headlines about unusual incidents or criticism of some aspect of the way American aviation is run can be very hard on a fearful flier's perspective. Some weeks when you read the paper you get the distinct impression that the sky may not be falling but everything in it is just about to.

But the reporters who pounce on foul-ups and dig for the inside stories on the system, the congresspeople who unmercifully grill FAA officials at hearings, the aviation experts who scream bloody murder to the press if they uncover potential problems, the analysts who seem to be impossible to satisfy about aviation safety—they're all my heroes. The harder to please they are, the better I like it. It would make me extremely nervous if these people were saying, "Oh, we figure the system's just about safe enough, let's just all relax and stop making such a big deal about it." The system can *always* be safer, and I'm glad the experts seem to be almost as paranoid about it as I am.

So I'm all for giving aviation front-page importance, but since you're not likely to read anything tomorrow morning about the sixteen thousand flights that took off and landed uneventfully today, I thought you might be interested in hearing a little bit about how the system *usually* works. I am going to be very presumptuous, here, and attempt to give you a few snapshots of an enormously complicated, multibillion-dollar network that employs millions of people and about which multiple controversies roil like the inside of an active volcano. You understand I had to leave a few things out. Perhaps I will put them in *White Knuckles,* Volumes II–MCXVI.

You'll notice even in this bare-bones overview that at every level there is an awfully lot of backing up, countersigning, repetition, triple-checking, and quadruple-redundancy, just like in this sentence only even more. This obsession with safety built into the routine is fine with me, but my first question is, if flying's not dangerous, what is everybody so worried about?

A noted psychologist who wrote a book about phobias suggests that the fear of heights is so deeply ingrained in the human species that it is reflected even in the operation and regulation of the airline industry.

The fear of losing tens of millions of dollars is probably just as deeply ingrained in the airline industry.

I hate to sound cynical, I'm sure the airline people are wonderful folks, but let us recognize that, as corporations, they take a keen interest in preventing accidents, and not just for humanitarian reasons, either. A very serious accident can cost an airline between $50–100 million in aircraft damage alone, perhaps another $50 million in survivors' claims, not to mention the enormous costs of investigating causes and making any necessary changes, paying legal fees, and suffering disastrous public relations. Manufacturers are often held accountable, too. Some estimates of the amounts plaintiffs will be seeking from the Boeing Company as a result of the 1985 Japan Air Lines 747 crash go as high as $1 billion.

But quite apart from the rare, catastrophic accident, airlines in the highly competitive post-deregulation market lose money and business when mechanical problems cause flight delays or keep a plane out of service, or the FAA is displeased enough to take action. Lately, sensitive to criticism that federal budget cuts and a burgeoning airline industry have diminished its ability to keep tabs on all airlines, the FAA has responded by coming down harder than ever on rule-benders—record seven-figure fines have been levied, airlines have been grounded (about sixty in 1985, none large), crews have been suspended (fifty-nine copilots at a commuter airline were deprived of their licenses in one fell swoop in 1986). The FAA has an understandable interest in publicizing its aggressiveness, and punitive actions can cost an airline almost as much in public confidence as they do in fine-payment.

As they should, to the mind of *this* airline passenger. I certainly don't mention this because I think any of us should feel particularly sorry for airlines. I guess I just have a healthy all-American appreciation of money as a motive. I feel better knowing the design and maintenance of passenger planes is not conducted on a let-your-conscience-be-your-guide basis. Since I have a lot at stake, I am glad the manufacturers and operators of airliners do, too.

Now that I've thoroughly maligned the airline industry's tender human feelings, let's look briefly at the system producing and operating airlines.[1]

The first links in the chain are the manufacturers, who are responsible for designing, building, and testing the planes, so that they meet the exacting requirements both of the customer airlines and of the FAA. After each plane is sold—and no matter how many times it's resold or how long it stays in service—the manufacturers are responsible for keeping track of its service history. And they are responsible for advising the airlines precisely how to maintain and operate the plane (if you would like a copy of the manufacturer's manuals for, say, a 747, you should allow shelf space for about a dozen Bible-sized flight manuals and about two dozen maintenance volumes, and the continuous updates during one year will run you about another $10,000).

The major manufacturers of airliners in this country are Boeing (various models of the 727 through 767s), McDonnell Douglas (DC-8, -9, and -10 series), and Lockheed (L-1011s), each of whom manufactures a lot of other kinds of planes and assorted hardware. This trio of American manufacturers has produced about 90 percent of the non-Communist world's airliners. A European consortium, Airbus, makes the highly sophisticated A-300s and A-310s, also in fairly wide use by U.S. carriers.

The consistent technological excellence of the modern airliners rolling off these assembly lines is probably the single point on which you will find nearly universal agreement among aviation experts.

After the lengthy, years-long design process, but about two years before a new airline model is certified for regular service, a few planes are taken at random right off the assembly line, to undergo the thousands of tests which must be performed before any plane of that type can be used as an air carrier.

The manufacturers do two things with these planes: fly them, and *pretend* to fly them.

Probably five or so will be flown, by test pilots from the manufacturer and the FAA, five days a week for about ten months. During that time they will be severely stalled, dived at high speed, rolled, fluttered, taken off and landed with their tails dragging and sparks flying, brought to shrieking halts at full takeoff speed to create brake fires, and otherwise flown in flamboyant disregard of normal practice. Virtually every sys-

tem onboard will be tested, and then turned off in midair and the plane
tested without it. The planes are operated as far beyond their certified
performance capabilities as humanly possible. A former Boeing test
flight engineer told me he didn't mind most of the maneuvers, but there
was one, which involved moving the plane very rapidly back and forth
at the same time it was rolling to one side, that invariably made him
sick, so on the days that maneuver was scheduled, he learned to bring
along a cup.

Those planes will eventually be sold to operators and fly out their
normal service lives less strenuously, but the test planes on the ground
are doomed. They are taken apart, and strung up piece by piece. On the
"static" rigs, they will just hang there, being systematically stressed—
hacked, bent, flexed, pulled—until they break. On the "fatigue" rigs,
the airframes will be subjected to the same vibrations, movements, and
strains of actual flight. One takeoff, pressurization, climb, cruise, descent, depressurization, and landing is considered a "cycle," and the
entire process can be simulated on the fatigue rig in about two and a
half minutes. The airframe will undergo probably about 100,000 of
these cycles—or the equivalent of some forty years in flight (the fatigue
rig is typically working on the test airframe twenty-four hours a day, six
days a week). Most of the major components will be fatigue-tested sepa-
rately. The testing for the 757's landing gear, for example, comprised
310,000 landings—about six normal landing-gear lifetimes.

The summary above is a pretty tiny slice of the entire developmental
and certification test procedures. At one point during 1982, when both
the 757 and the 767 were being tested, Boeing's flight test engineering
department alone employed over nine hundred people. I would love to
give you fifty examples of the kind of torture inflicted on airplane components; for some morbid reason this systematic cruelty to the planes
that have served me so faithfully fascinates me. But I'll restrain myself
to one.

The DC-8 was expected to be in service for twenty years. While it
was being tested, one of the forward fuselages was fatigue-cycled for the
equivalent of 112 years. After this century or so, the engineers–inquisi-
tors wanted to find out if the fuselage might have developed some hid-
den weaknesses, so they pressurized it to simulate flight, and then repeatedly harpooned it with a fifteen-inch-wide blade. The engineers

were pretty fatigued after this exercise, but no weaknesses were discovered in the fuselage.

And so, eventually, the model is certified, after the FAA is satisfied that the planes will perform reliably into future generations. The DC-3 was designed over fifty years ago, long before computers and the rest of manufacturers' current gear, and many DC-3s are still in regular service. In fact, as of 1985 the all-time record for total airframe hours was held by a DC-3, still in service, at over eighty-seven thousand hours, the equivalent of ten solid years in the air.

Now the planes are sold to airlines, who become responsible for maintaining and operating them. And if you're worried you drew the only lemon off the assembly line, each and every plane sold has also been flight-tested several times, by the manufacturer, the FAA, and the airline customer. So that stolid old workhorse you're flying has seen a little aerial excitement in its day.

The new planes come with the manufacturers' detailed instructions—exactly how the plane is designed to perform in every situation. The FAA also hands the airline an enormous document called the MRB (for Maintenance Review Board), outlining the initial requirements for the plane's maintenance. Each airline operates differently, however—some specialize in long hauls, for instance, and some in short hops, conditions which will affect the plane's upkeep necessities—so the carrier will negotiate its own custom-tailored program with the FAA. The airline's program must be at least as stringent as the MRB.

The manufacturers and the airlines base their maintenance routines around three basic concepts, depending on the part, and on when the plane was certified: "safe life" means a part has been given a designated "lifetime" and so the maintenance plan has to provide for replacing it long before that time; "fail-safe" means even if the part *does* break, another part can take over and safety won't be affected; and, since 1978, the working philosophy has been "damage tolerance," which means everyone assumes the part will become damaged somehow and it must be able to operate safely, while damaged, for a considerable time *after* its malfunction would become noticeable enough for repair. A crack, for instance, cannot cause a problem even if it went undiscovered until it was so big that even my car's mechanic would notice it.

When malfunctions become noticeable, of course, they're fixed. After each flight, the crew enters in the log book anything that has to be fixed or checked. Some items can wait until scheduled maintenance—but only if they're on a special list approved by the FAA, called a Minimum Equipment List. If they're not on the list, the plane can't legally fly unless they're in working order.

But the objective is to fix problems *before* something breaks. As a broad generalization, a plane will typically undergo "A" inspections, a mechanic visually checking everything over, about every three hundred flight hours; a more complex "B" check at perhaps one thousand hours; and a "C" check every three thousand hours, which will probably be once a year, when panels are removed and sections taken apart and inspection specialists comb the structure as if they were looking for drugs. The "C" check will probably take a couple of days. Somewhere around fifteen thousand hours, the "D" check will remove the plane from service for an extended period while it is virtually taken apart and put back together again, and any major structural changes or refurbishing are performed at that time.

In between these milestones, planes are being checked before and after each flight by crews and ground mechanics, including a mandatory "walk-around" by a crew member who knows what to look for before the flight. Tire treads are being measured and fluid levels monitored. The engines are being tracked by computer during the flight, so that any deviations from standard performance can be spotted before they add up to trouble. Various other parts and components are arriving at their scheduled replacement times, whether they've given any trouble or not. And assorted special inspections are being performed, according to the kind of work the individual plane does, and to give the technicians a chance to practice all the digital computing, X-ray detecting, crack-management, and residual strength analyses they learned in school. Every repair, replacement, or inspection of any part of an airplane must be signed for by the technicians performing the work, and then checked and countersigned by at least one supervisor.

If something on a plane wears out or breaks in an unexpected way, the airlines fill out a Service Difficulty Report (SDR) which goes to the FAA and to the manufacturers and other interested parties. You could arrange, at considerable expense, to regularly receive these, also, if you are a wealthy fan of monumentally boring reading. The manufacturers compile and monitor SDRs, and will advise all operators worldwide if they spot some untoward trend. They'll send out a Service Bulletin. The overwhelming majority of these are only interesting if you're trying to run an airline on time. For example, only about 6 percent of the bulletins Lockheed has issued on the L-1011 have been safety-related enough to include some time limit on compliance. Only about 1 percent have been classified as "alert" bulletins, for which the time limit is usually "now."

The FAA has to approve the technical specifications on most significant Service Bulletins. Once in a while, if the FAA considers a matter particularly pressing, they'll get into the act themselves and issue an Airworthiness Directive, which has the force of law.

By now you are probably suspecting that I intend to give *you* a federal examination on airplane maintenance. So let's caption this snapshot and move on. The caption is: Not *one* passenger fatality in the United States has ever resulted from a jet transport accident in which metal fatigue or corrosion was cited by the NTSB as a cause or even a related factor. Maintenance or structural problems in general have been the cause of one fatal jet transport accident in the United States in the last twenty-five years, and less than 4 percent of passenger jet accidents worldwide—nine accidents total.

The final stop on our whirlwind tour of airliner operation is the national air traffic control system. This part of the system certainly gets its share of bad press, possibly because it doesn't get much press at all unless it screws up. I didn't come here to praise it or to bury it. I only want to give you a little general perspective, since if you read the papers you're liable to be convinced the airlines routinely turn their exquisitely engineered, exhaustively maintained, expertly piloted aircraft over to a bunch of people on the verge of nervous breakdowns.

The first time I visited an air traffic control center I fully expected to find a huge room full of frenzied, chain-smoking, quivering basket cases, fingernails bitten to the quick, narrowly averting aviation tragedies every few seconds, muttering, "Whew, that was a close one." At the Leesburg, Virginia, Regional Center, which handles sectors from New York to Florida (the busiest air corridor in the world), my guide kept saying, "Here, move closer, look at this," and I was *afraid* to get any closer to an actual, real-life air traffic controller in action. I was sure he would glance up from his duties to say hello and five blips would disappear from the radar screen.

Naturally, when I calmed down enough to pay attention, I saw what you would see if you visited a typical air traffic control center or airport tower—a huge room full of highly trained professionals following exacting procedures and operating some truly spectacular space-age technology. Nationwide, controllers are performing some two hundred thousand distinct "operations"—takeoffs, landings, flights through a sector, etc.—a day for commercial and private planes.

It's hard to get to be a traffic controller, and then it's harder still to stay one. About 50 percent of trainees wash out before they even graduate from the academy, located in Oklahoma City. The FAA is currently trying to refine its screening techniques to reduce that number a little, but in general, the academy is *trying* to pressure candidates to their limits, so they can weed out people who can't take pressure. (People like me, for instance, who are overstressed by Pac-Man.) During a controller's training and long apprenticeship—usually a total of three to four years—every error is carefully noted, and after a certain number the candidate's air traffic control career is finished before it starts, although, to take advantage of the training already invested, he might be reassigned to some other noncontroller job in the system. And even if a controller has been on the job for twenty years, he or she (the number of women is increasing in a formerly virtually all-male profession) still must complete a minimum of two hours per week continuing training and one week per year of special proficiency courses on the simulator.

Typically, the most senior controllers, who get paid the most, are assigned to the busiest airports and sectors. A controller spends about two hours at a stretch actively directing traffic, and during the busiest times, a team of two or three controllers will be working at each screen. The precise arrangement varies, of course. A controller on the midnight watch in Seattle could probably sit there calmly by himself for two or three hours. A controller on the midnight watch in Indianapolis would be very busy, indeed, directing the planes carrying packages that absolutely, positively had to get there overnight, and he might only sit at the screen for an hour at a time. I decided, on my tour, that I'd better point out the fact that computers occasionally break down, and might just break down at the busiest possible air traffic moment. My guide thanked me for the helpful suggestion, but allowed as how they'd already thought of that. If the main computer system goes haywire, a second complete system kicks in, and if the entire computer goes *completely* out of whack, each active controller is fully certified to guide airplanes without the help of radar. Non-radar controlling, in fact, is one of the first skills trainee controllers master.

Beginning early in his training, long before a controller is assigned to "live traffic," he has been working on traffic problems of steadily advancing complexity. The tests are generally built on actual situations from a particular day's traffic, and the candidate is working with the same equipment the active controllers are using, except that the "pretend" situations are electronically flagged so the computer will know the difference between made-up emergencies and real ones. Because, in addition to routine operations, an advanced student (like the active controllers in their retraining exercises) is working with simulated situations that might combine several planes taking off and landing at the same time while several more are holding and one loses its radio and one experiences an in-flight emergency and another one is being hijacked. I've just chosen a few from long lists of eventualities the controller is required to practice until he or she can instantly recognize them and deal with them effectively.

Without an error. You and I can pretty much camouflage most of our work errors. If an air traffic controller makes an error, the computer, the other controllers, the supervisors on the floor, and the pilots involved know immediately, even if the error is technical and relatively minor, because errors must be corrected within *seconds*. The FAA department in charge of the system is informed; errors are painstakingly counted and analyzed. And the rest of us probably read about it in the papers the next day. I suppose if I were an air traffic controller's mother I might consider this inflexible scrutiny unfair, but I'm not and I like the scrutiny just fine.

You and I have one simple interest in the matter of air traffic control —how safely it works—but you should remember that some of the criticism of the "inadequate" air traffic control system is not really about safety, although it's almost invariably couched that way. Some of the complaints are mainly about money. One of the primary ways the FAA has assured safe operations with fewer controllers is to limit the

number of flights, which is not altogether popular with an airline industry trying to serve record numbers of passengers and turn a profit in the
ferociously competitive deregulated marketplace. I'm afraid I will have
to disqualify myself from making any comments on this financial side of
the question. If it were up to me, planes would be allowed into the sky
one at a time. When that one landed, another one could take off. An
MBA I'm not.

Now, let us get off the subject of air traffic controllers before we are
hit by flying brickbats.

If you're nervous about entrusting your life to strangers, you should
try to keep in mind that each of those strangers is backed up every
moment he or she is on the job by a huge and hypervigilant system. You
also might be interested in knowing that your *worrying* is also being
backed up by a system. There are entire organizations that worry about
airline aviation safety for a living. Just a few of the major ones:

▪ The Air Line Pilots Association. ALPA has about thirty-four thousand pilot members, and active on-line pilots serve as safety representatives from each of ALPA's forty-nine member airlines. Whatever pilots
do to ensure their *own* safety generally benefits the rest of the people on
the plane, and ALPA is extremely active in pressuring Congress, the
FAA, and their own airlines on safety issues they consider important.
Just the summaries of ALPA's current ongoing safety projects fill a
large three-ring binder, but a few areas they're involved in include airport safety standards, all-weather flying, accident survival, charting and
instrument procedures, human performance factors, pilot training, and
providing working-pilot input throughout the process of designing and
certifying airliners and equipment. ALPA also conducts its own accident investigations, and they have a special hot line number so that the
entire organization can quickly bring its considerable resources to bear
if a pilot spots potentially unsafe practices, in his or her own company,
or anywhere in the system at large.

▪ The Aviation Consumer Action Project. I think it's fair to say this
nonprofit organization, one of the consumer action groups that comprise the Public Citizen Corporation founded by Ralph Nader, looks at
the FAA and the airlines with a fairly critical eye. Watches them like a
starving hawk would probably be more accurate. Just recently, ACAP
has been involved—with other organizations, and successfully, in their

view—in efforts to change the way the FAA counts and reports safety statistics, to improve the medical equipment airlines carry onboard, and to keep U.S. airlines from following the example of some foreign carriers by closing off one or more emergency exits from wide-bodied jets. ALPA and the Association of Flight Attendants were also major players in the latter action.* One of ACAP's current projects is an idea that would make it possible for airline passengers to compare the records of various airlines by a number of "performance indicators," such as pilot experience, money spent on maintenance programs, and so forth. Needless to say, putting together such a "chart," and doing it fairly, would be an incredibly complicated enterprise. The idea is controversial in the extreme, so you'd have to ask ACAP directly how they envision the plan would work.

▪ The Flight Safety Foundation. Their 450 members in fifty-four countries include most of the major airline transport companies in the free world. Their mission is to study flight safety technology and act as a source of objective information about the state of the art. FSF publishes a variety of bulletins and technical digests, and conducts major seminars on air safety issues. They also perform independent, confidential Aviation Safety Audits of individual operations.

▪ The National Transportation Safety Board. Responsible, among other activities, for the exhaustive official investigations of aircraft accidents and significant incidents, the NTSB makes recommendations about safety improvements not only in their accident reports but throughout the year. Probably nobody in the world has a more intimate knowledge of what can go wrong with an airplane than an accident investigator, whether he or she is from the NTSB or any of the other organizations which study plane crashes in the minutest technical detail. "Kicking tin" is the common phrase among investigators for sorting through the wreckage of an aviation disaster. I figure if *those* people are still traveling by air (and most of them do a lot more flying than any of us) after what they've seen and know, maybe I can afford to, as well.

Although I have not run across any accident investigators who have flight phobias, neither have I met one who did not have a profound respect for the importance of constant safety vigilance, so in that sense,

---

* To be fair, I'll note that the foreign carriers proved to the satisfaction of their own governing authorities that removing the exits wouldn't compromise safety.

"fear of flying" pervades not only these organizations, but the FAA, the congressional subcommittees, the safety offices and engineering departments within each plane manufacturer, each component manufacturer, and each airline, and all the other organizations, universities, and private research companies I've shamefully neglected.

I have given you a few addresses in the back of the book. If you're interested in hearing more about how these people work for your safety, or if you'd just like to remind them you're relying on *them* to keep a healthy fear of flying so that you don't have to keep yours, write them a letter. If every fearful flier in America wrote a letter to his or her congressman, I don't think we'd have much trouble with FAA budgets, but let's keep my grandiose political visions out of this.

I'm only suggesting that once we get on a plane there is not much need for you and I to add our uninformed amateur compulsions to the already prodigious professional total. We can conserve our raw courage for times when we have to rely on less carefully supervised strangers such as lovers and cab drivers.

And I suppose those of us who worry about the system should remember the example of the man who went into the airspace with no system at all. Lord knows that is the *only* sense in which this man's deeply silly aerial foray could be considered exemplary.[2]

He was apparently hard up for entertainment one California summer day in 1982 and decided to pursue what he later said had been a dream of his since he was thirteen. He was now thirty-three but his idea of a really neato time apparently had not changed very much in the interim. He attached a bunch of large helium balloons to an aluminum lawn chair so that he could sit comfortably as he was borne aloft. I shouldn't say he had no system, he had friends who were supposed to hold on to the rope tethering him loosely to earth while he tried out his idea, and he had a BB gun with which he was going to shoot out the balloons when he wanted to come down. But the flight went from experimental to operational a little faster than he'd expected. His friends made a slight controller error and didn't hold on to the rope.

The air chair itself was performing flawlessly. Exceeding its design expectations, in fact. Getting up to about 16,000 feet, in fact. I certainly wouldn't trust the pressurization system on any of *my* lawn chairs at that altitude, but admittedly I'm sort of a weenie about oxygen deprivation. Perhaps the mental faculties of the gentleman in question didn't require much fuel to burn at their customary level. He shot out a balloon or two before he experienced a major landing system malfunction when he dropped his BB gun. Or you might call it pilot error. I think if I were going to write a ballad about this man I would call it "I've Been Suffering from Pilot Error Since the Day I Was Born."

Pilots on airliners taking off from Los Angeles International Airport noticed, off in the distance, a—a what? Is it a bird? Is it a plane? Is it a lawn chair attached to helium balloons carrying a chilly fun-seeker? And gradually calls began coming in to the FAA office at Long Beach, no doubt leading the operators to wonder whether they should plug the callers straight through to the extraterrestrial kidnappings department. But it so happened that this Inexcusable Flying Object was now being operated—sort of—in the same sector as the Long Beach National Airport, a quite large and busy airport, an airport where very little of the traffic is proceeding at the leisurely speed of a lawn chair. The Long Beach control tower spotted it, and the authorities quickly became convinced that not *all* the controllers could be having the exact same bizarre hallucination as the citizens of Long Beach–San Pedro. Eventually the lawn chair came down, as lawn chairs will, and was met, as it crash-landed into somebody's backyard, by distinctly unamused officials. The guy wasn't hurt. Well, maybe his feelings were hurt.

The FAA has very little sense of humor about the national airspace, nor would I if I had been on a jet landing or taking off from Long Beach Airport that day. I have enough to worry about without considering the consequences of a midair collision with a lawn chair, although on balance it probably would've been harder on him than on me. This appears to be only one of a number of possibilities that did not occur to our perchance not-entirely-zipped aviation pioneer. They charged him with Operating an Aircraft Without an Airworthiness Certificate, Failing to Maintain Contact with a Control Tower, and a few other things, and eventually settled, after lengthy litigation, for fining him $1,500. If they'd had a regulation on the books for Acting Out Your All-Time Stupidest Idea, he'd have been put away for life.

But the next time you get scared flying along in your multimillion-dollar airliner, remember, it could be worse. You could be flying along in a lawn chair.

Worst Cases

You may not want to know any more about plane crashes than you already know. If you think it will scare you out of even going *near* a plane if you read about a few of the times when a great many things went disastrously wrong with the system all at once, well, maybe you should skip this section. You certainly won't read any of this in an airline's in-flight magazine, any more than you're likely to see *Airport* or any of its sequels screened on your flight to Hawaii. Airlines probably wouldn't even bring up the part about the oxygen masks if the FAA didn't make them.

You can hardly blame them. They have provided, at no small expense, a nice safe plane and a smart, skillful crew, so why get everybody all worked up over something that has a chance in the range of .00001 percent of happening?*

A former accident investigator, now a technical expert at a major safety organization, told me he didn't think people wanted to know "the bad stuff." He said he was waiting for a flight once, and the announcement came that the flight had been delayed because of mechanical difficulties. When an airline representative walked into the gate area, one

---

* Every year, over 99.99999 percent of Part 121 (large, commercial) airline flights are completed without a single fatality. In recent years, the number has often been 100 percent. In an unusually bad year, the far right digit may fluctuate slightly: in 1985, the number was approximately 99.99992.

person asked what exactly the mechanical difficulty *was*. According to my friend the expert, a chorus of cries from the other waiting passengers went up, "No! Don't tell us! We don't want to know!" The agent didn't tell them, and eventually they all piled on the plane and flew uneventfully and none the wiser to their destination.

I'll bet I know who the fearful flier in *that* bunch was. The guy who asked the question. Call us worrywarts, call us masochists—I prefer to call us relentless truth-seekers—we may not *want* to know, but we feel we must.

What you will *not* find in this chapter are the kind of hair-raising plane crash stories that usually start out with "The drizzle had just begun when John Smith kissed his new bride good-bye, neither knowing that he was seventy-five minutes away from a rendezvous with Fate." My advice is, don't read those until you've been over your fear of flying for a couple of years. Writers aren't a particularly brilliant lot, in my experience, but one thing they know how to do very well is get emotional mileage out of a rendezvous with Fate, no matter if it's Hank Aaron stepping up to the plate or a genuine human tragedy of any kind. I certainly think that's a job, however strange, that's worth doing (I'm a little prejudiced), but when it comes to flying, your emotions are already in a pretty volatile state.

Though it may sound contradictory, the information in this chapter about accidents and emergencies (and situations that *look* like emergencies but aren't) is meant to make you feel safer. Almost every fearful flier I've ever talked to has told me he or she always felt compelled to listen to every word written or broadcast about an airplane accident. They couldn't help themselves, they often said. One graduate of U.S. Air's Fearful Flyers Program told me, about news reports of crashes, "Oh, I used to *feed* off that stuff."

I did, too. Stare long and hard at the photographs. Read every name of the dead. Stoke my fear like a furnace.

Whatever this compulsion is—the ordinary morbid curiosity that motivates rubberneckers at bad car wrecks; an understandable reaction to the sometimes melodramatic press coverage of all disasters; a sort of negative magic whereby if you suffer enough over *their* tragedy, maybe you can avert yours; or simple human pity and wonder—if you are a fearful flier you cannot afford to allow yourself to be swamped by what you know or think you know about plane crashes.

This chapter is brief, and I'll tell you exactly what's in it so you can decide if you're more like the man who asked the nature of the difficulty or the people who didn't want to know (either position is perfectly understandable):

1. Facts about some recent accidents, and what the system did about them.

2. An alternative way to read about plane crashes.

3. A little information about how you could handle yourself if you were faced with an emergency while you were on a plane (*many* more people have survived airplane accidents than have not).

For those still with me, herewith, the bad stuff.

THE BEST—AND WORST—OF TIMES

First, let's define terms. I am focusing on major U.S. airlines, flying big jets, in this country, on regularly scheduled passenger flights, which I assume represents the kind of flying you do most. I don't mean to suggest in any way that other kinds of flying are inherently dangerous. Regional airlines, commuter airlines, charter airlines, most foreign airlines, cargo airlines, and private aviation (some corporate business jets are equipped with technology so advanced it's not even in wide use by airlines yet) all have excellent safety records.[1] But, as you recall, I'm trying to save some material for my next hundreds of books.

For the kind of planes I'm talking about, the decade before 1985 was, on balance, the safest in aviation history, a logical—and continuing—culmination of years of experience with jets and steady improvements in technology. In Appendix III in the back of the book, I've listed every fatal accident from 1974 to 1985, in the category we're discussing. As you can see, between 1980 and 1985 particularly there were two long stretches of near-perfect safety records—no fatalities in 1980, 1981, 1983, or 1984. The August 1985 Dallas tragedy was the first fatal American jet accident in two years for a major airline. The first for Delta, a recognized industry leader in safety standards, in over a decade. The first ever at the Dallas–Fort Worth International Airport, the fourth-busiest in the United States, in eleven years of operation. And the second in the flying history of the Lockheed L-1011. Of the 250 L-1011s manufactured since the first was built in 1968, all but a few are still in regular service around the world, and the single other fatal accident occurred in 1972; the plane itself was not a factor, and was not cited as a factor in the Dallas disaster.

But sadly and a bit ironically, the crashes whose images haunt us most also occurred during this same safe decade. Even the place names can call up those terrifying images. Tenerife, the worst aviation accident ever. San Diego. Washington, D.C. Chicago. New Orleans.

I would never suggest that these images are worse than the reality. We will never know that reality, and speculating about it is painful and presumptuous.

All we *do* know is that *those conditions are not identical to the conditions on your flight.* No matter if it's blizzarding or thunderstorming or you're taking off from the same airport, no matter what other superficial similarities you might worry over.

For two basic reasons. First, most modern accidents are the result of a highly unlikely *combination* of factors, even the worst of which might not have been irreparable had it not been compounded by many others. A slight change in even one of the circumstances would have dramatically altered, perhaps prevented altogether, the result.

Accident reports are filled with "if only's." The plane that crashed as it took off or landed has almost always been immediately preceded by similar planes taking off or landing safely under apparently similar conditions. At New Orleans International Airport on July 9, 1982, four air carriers and a general aviation plane departed safely between 3:58 and 4:27. TWA 759 crashed at 4:08. The accident scenarios pieced together so painstakingly by investigators almost always admit possible alternatives. The engines of Southern Airways 242 were overwhelmed by a massive ingestion of water and hail in a severe thunderstorm minutes before landing on April 4, 1977, causing engine damage so severe and unusual that the NTSB investigators could find "no other recorded instance of a transport category turbojet aircraft experiencing a similar emergency." Yet even at that point, the report noted, when some kind of accident was probably inevitable, the plane remained to some extent controllable, and if it had continued just long enough to get (as the pilot was apparently making an effort to do) to the long runways at nearby Dobbins Air Force Base, perhaps . . .

Virtually every accident report reads much the same way. Experts group accidents together to analyze their general causes—human errors, weather, mechanical failures—and to better characterize what happens in crashes—speeds, impacts, angles, damage patterns—but the specific web of causes and effects is always unique. So the reoccurrence of the precise freak combination of factors that caused any one accident is already unlikely in the extreme.

Still, accident investigators do not take a mystical view of plane crashes. Something very specific went wrong. Within minutes the site is swarmed over by investigators, not only from the NTSB, but also, among the many who will be involved, specialists from the FAA, the manufacturers, ALPA, and the airline. I spoke with a Delta captain who landed his scheduled flight at Dallas–Fort Worth eight minutes ahead of the Dallas crash. He was immediately reassigned on the spot to help begin the investigation. The government and airline procedures following an accident are exhaustive. A final accident report will comprise hundreds of documents, based on over a year's worth of interviews, technical and forensic studies, expert testimony, and the careful physical analysis of every inch of the plane in question. The summaries alone often run to 100 pages. Even then, the conclusions will be carefully labeled *"Probable* Causes." And the study continues. Long after reports are issued, they are often revised to include new information (please keep that in mind as you read the deceptively brief notations of major contributing factors in Appendix III at the back of this book).

So, in addition to the tiny chance that the same set of coincidences might converge once again, the second reason accidents seldom "repeat" themselves is that every accident sets off a giant wave of corrections, countermeasures, changes in procedure, and, often, changes in the planes. The investigators find the technical circumstances which allowed an accident. Occasionally they also find related circumstances which could, conceivably, allow another accident, perhaps an entirely different one. Whatever can be fixed, is fixed. Not just a specific part or procedure, but the complex net of surrounding factors.

Sometimes the "fix" takes a long time. Microbursts, for example, recur in accident annals, and represent a particularly difficult problem because the solution—short of changing Mother Nature—involves so many factors: detection, for which the technology is only now becoming available; rapid, reliable communication from the forecasters to the controllers and pilots; and perfecting the actions that humans then take with the information, also a capability that has been much improved in recent years, but which depends in turn on detection and communication. Even in this case, however, since a 1975 New York accident focused attention on microburst phenomena, the science for dealing with them has grown by quantum leaps.

But, invariably, long before massive "solutions" can be tested and instituted, new precautions spread throughout the entire system very quickly. Inspections of the worldwide fleet of similar models may be the first step. Pan Am, TWA, United, and Northwest Orient, the four major U.S. operators of 747s, began special inspections of their fleets within days of the 1985 Japan Air Lines crash, and many such inspections followed, becoming more and more specific as more was learned about the accident. In the aftermath of the 1979 Chicago O'Hare crash, the worst disaster in American commercial aviation history, the DC-10 became probably the most exhaustively inspected airplane in history.

As of this writing, the official causes in the Japan Air Lines accident have not yet been established, but a number of precautionary changes have already been ordered throughout the worldwide fleet. A change may seem minor; for instance, a cover plate has now been placed on a small access door in the 747's tail, a modification that costs around $200 per plane. But it may have been pressurized air exploding through that small opening after a damaged wall collapsed that led to large portions of the tail and the hydraulic control systems being destroyed. One small link might have altered the long, terrible chain of events.

In the case of the Chicago DC-10 accident, the major fault turned out to be in a widely used (now, of course, eliminated) but improperly performed maintenance technique, a fault undetected earlier because, once again, an unusual chain of events was necessary to stress the parts involved sufficiently to culminate in disastrous failure. The accident report cites "intolerance of a prescribed operational procedure to this unique emergency." But all DC-10s were also modified so that the wing control surfaces would remain operational even under the same critical circumstances, and engine brackets were redesigned to make them less susceptible to any kind of maintenance damage.

Further, the damage to the left wing caused when the engine separated had resulted in a stall of that wing, but there were indications that, had some of the warning systems remained functional, a compensation for the plane's sudden lack of lift on one side could have been made, and the plane, though badly damaged, would still probably have been able to recover. So the backups for those warning systems were improved, too. And takeoff procedures for *all* aircraft were modified, to build in an extra margin of climb speed—added time and power for recovery from a stall.

Besides specific procedural or mechanical changes, the investigation of an accident will often have even more far-reaching effects on the system. After the San Diego Pacific Southwest Airlines crash, an entirely new way of controlling the airspace around large airports was instituted, and although those limits have worked well in the years since, the 1986 Aeromexico accident will probably influence a wide range of new boundary safeguards at terminal control areas across the country. After a 1972 crash in the Florida Everglades when an accidental and unnoticed disengagement of the autopilot occurred (the crew apparently was preoccupied with a faulty warning light; and there also had been problems with the way the autopilot was installed), autopilots were universally equipped with warning systems so they could not be disengaged unintentionally.

Perhaps the most dramatic example of system-wide changes resulting from an accident followed the 1974 crash in northern Virginia, outside Dulles International Airport, one of the major airports in the Washington, D.C., area. The accident report cited among the contributing factors an apparent miscommunication between the pilot and the air traffic controller, and an inadequacy of the applicable charts for the region. The plane was flying normally, and the crew was unaware of any danger, as the approach clearance was given about forty miles from the airport, but the descent to 1,800 feet, although perhaps justifiable for the situation as understood by the crew, brought the plane into collision with a hill outside the airport.

After that, the Ground Proximity Warning System in planes and the

Minimum Safe Altitude Warning System on the ground were universally adopted. NASA established the Aviation Safety Reporting System, a national, confidential hot line for users of the airspace, to report potentially unsafe conditions or incidents that indicate problems with the system (there had been previous complaints about the approach charts for the Dulles area at that time). And routine approach procedures followed by pilots and by controllers were changed. Planes approaching airports for landing no longer may immediately descend to the minimum allowed altitude, but must proceed by carefully designated stages.

(Dulles International Airport, I should note, is consistently rated by pilots as among the best, from a safety standpoint, in the country.)

You might conclude by examples of this kind that the system in general waits around for a tragic accident before anything gets changed, and you would not be the first to level such a charge. You might also take the less harsh view that the system can absorb so many mistakes by its inherent soundness that subtle weaknesses do not become visible until an unlikely number of coincidences cluster precisely at a vulnerable point. And many changes—even large-scale improvements, such as the new computer capabilities now coming on-line in air traffic control centers—are made as a result not of accidents but of new research, service histories, noninjury incidents, or industry analyses.

Whatever view you took, you could find ample evidence to support your case. The only statistic you would have a difficult time finding is the number of lives that have been saved by a particular measure. It would likely be a very large number, but it could also be zero, if the exact circumstances never repeated in the identical sequence again. There's little way of predicting, for example, if the fire extinguishers on your plane will someday save hundreds of lives, or will hang unused in their compartments throughout all the uneventful years of the plane's service. But thousands of changes and improvements over many years have made the system as safe as it is.

Certainly, on every airline flight that takes off anywhere in this country, the crew is trained and the plane is equipped to face: emergencies that happened years before, under entirely different conditions; emergencies that have never happened, but might, under certain unusual conditions; and emergencies that, God willing, will never happen anywhere, under any conditions. And I wouldn't feel safe with any less, because I have a simple criterion for accident prevention: if a measure saves only *one* life, I consider it amply worthwhile, because that is exactly how many lives I have.

By the way, that's one of the reasons I've given you so many addresses in Appendix IV. If that's your criterion, too, I don't think it hurts to bring that to the attention of the powers-that-be every once in a while.

Improvements are being made continually. Very recently, new standards for fire resistance in seat coverings and cabin furnishings have been established, and special floor markings required to lead passengers to exits if smoke obscures vision at eye level. Anything that slows the spread of fire in the cabin, or helps people evacuate faster, has an enormous potential for saving lives, since post-crash fires (in the majority of cases, smoke and toxic fume inhalation) have caused about 80 percent of accident fatalities.

And in the very near future, you can look forward to a number of other changes which are now moving out of the research centers and into airplanes, such as onboard Doppler radar units that can distinguish wind shears much more reliably, airborne threat-avoidance equipment, reinforced seat restraints, fuel that would be less likely to ignite after a crash. Yes, I know you probably saw a photo of the remote-controlled plane the FAA was using in 1985 to test a version of this fuel, called anti-misting kerosene, as the plane spectacularly caught fire during the test, but I told you about taking at face value everything you read in the paper. This experiment, called the Controlled Impact Demonstration (CID, affectionately known as Crash In the Desert) was not at all the quasicomical unmitigated failure the general press portrayed (if you're interested, see the Notes section).[2] A fuel that would reduce the incidence of catastrophic post-crash fire, and thus drastically reduce the number of fatalities, is still a distinct possibility.

I am, of course, pleased that planes will be even safer in the future, because I still have quite a few exotic places I would like to visit, and maybe by "the future" I'll be able to afford it, although I have my doubts. But in the meantime, the fact that research and experience constantly lead to new safety improvements means I'm already flying on about sixty years' worth. To tell you the truth, I would not have liked flying very much in the 1920s. The first airmail service lost thirty-one out of its first forty pilots to crashes; the entire takeoff section of the 1926 federal air commerce regulations had only this to say: "The take-off shall not be commenced until there is no risk of collision with land-ing aircraft and until preceding aircraft are clear of the field." Or in the forties, when a study concluded that flying was just about as safe as driving, and we all know how safe *that* is. Or in the fifties, before air traffic controllers had computers, and the basic safeguard against mid-air collisions was that the FAA sternly prohibited them. Or in the six-ties, when there was, on average, one fatal accident per month. I wasn't all that crazy about flying in the *seventies,* before I even *knew* that planes didn't have Ground Proximity Warning Systems. But most peo-ple who flew throughout those years never even experienced an incident worth telling their grandchildren about, and in the latter part of the 1980s, I can fly much more safely than any of the millions before me. In years to come, the margin for error will be reduced to an even tinier fraction.

Perhaps it will be possible, then, to eliminate accidents altogether?

Thinking About the Unthinkable

I sort of doubt it, don't you?

Planes have crashed, a small percentage with fatal result, and some-day, somewhere, another one will, and you will read about it, and you will think to yourself, "That's the most awful thing I can imagine and I'm *going* to be imagining it every time I step onto a plane if I ever can bring myself to do so again as long as I live."

Nothing can mitigate the horror of a bad plane crash. I must rely on you to understand that I have no intention of suggesting we can take such a tragedy lightly or callously. If we are human, we cannot.

You are in a special situation. You are particularly afraid of flying, and a deep fear like that can distort the way you connect flying acci-dents to your own experience. I would like to offer you just three ideas to consider:

1. Beware of jumping to conclusions ("I'll never fly at night again," for example, or "I'll never fly on that kind of plane again"). You do not

know, and are not likely to know for a long time, what exactly caused the accident, although the newspaper report is likely to cite *something* right away. The obvious answer is not always correct, and is never complete.

2. If you're worrying, "Gee, what if that could happen to me?", be assured that there are literally hundreds of professional investigators, thousands of pilots, scores of airlines, and a large federal agency worrying about exactly the same possibility. A lot of congressmen, too, but I don't know how reassuring you find that particular detail. They are asking the questions you are asking, and hundreds more you would ask if you had the time, training, resources, and technical expertise. If any detail of the accident could have a potential effect on other flights, they are the ones qualified to find it, and they will not keep quiet about it. Their job is raising hell about accidents.

3. The entire system has been galvanized. Controllers, maintenance supervisors, pilots, airlines, inspectors, they are all on red alert. Official lines of communication are in action, and so also are unofficial "grapevines." Luckily, changes will be built into the routine so that this heightened state of anxiety becomes institutionalized, but for now, you may be assured that if anyone was getting a little complacent, nobody is complacent now.

STAYING ALIVE

Boy, do I feel silly telling you what to do if you're in a plane crash, when we both know the chances are pretty slim you'll ever even be in an *emergency.* All right, so I'm overprotective. So sue me.

But you're *already* worrying about something that in all probability will never happen, and that kind of worrying has no conceivable payoff. If we're going to prepare, we might as well prepare constructively. Oh, dear. First I sound like a Jewish mother and now I sound like a schoolmarm.

People who are afraid to fly, and people who aren't, generally agree on one thing: if a plane *does* crash, that's it, everybody aboard is history, and not just aviation history. A study of airline passengers done for the

FAA† indicated that the average passenger believes 75 percent of plane crashes are fatal, and maybe 25 percent are not.³

In reality, *the exact opposite is true.* The Flight Safety Foundation found that, in about 86 percent of airplane accidents, *no one* is killed. In about 14 percent, the accident results in the death of someone onboard.

Technically, upward of 70 percent even of fatal accidents are classified as "survivable." The forces of impact were not necessarily beyond what a human being can withstand (this stands to reason, since the majority of accidents occur during takeoff or landing, at relatively low speeds), and the plane's structure remained intact enough for human survival (you already know how strong a plane is).

But there is, obviously, a big difference between "survivable" in that sense, and the confusion and turmoil that would face an ordinary person in the aftermath of an accident. A substantial body of research indicates that *panic* is a relatively unusual reaction. Much more often, people do not know or can't think what to do, and they sit in their seats until too late.

It gets to be too late pretty quick. While the passenger in most "routine" emergencies might have plenty of time for an orderly evacuation, in a bad accident there might only be a matter of minutes. Just long enough for a person to do what he or she is prepared to do, and that does not have to be "nothing."

A lady in one of Captain Tom Bunn's SOAR classes asked him if she would be safer sitting in the back of the plane. He patiently discussed the pros and cons with her—mostly dependent on knowing in advance exactly what kind of accident you're going to be in—but observed that worrying about where to sit on an airliner is a little bit as if someone offered you a million dollars, and you were delighted until they said they only wanted to keep one penny, at which point you said, "Then, never mind, keep your lousy $999,999.99."

But I'll still feel better knowing you know these things. Please humor me.

1. Listen to the safety briefing. Read the safety card.

It will only take a few minutes, as opposed to spending the entire

† The study was conducted by Dr. Daniel A. Johnson, a distinguished expert in accident survival, who wrote a wonderful book called *Just in Case,* which I'll tell you more about in the Notes section.

flight worrying, which is needlessly extravagant. The airline safety briefing is probably the most blatantly ignored safety precaution in modern life. I bet you pay more attention to the warning on plastic dry cleaning bags that THIS IS NOT A TOY. A legendary story at the NTSB goes that a flight attendant, fed up with doing her demonstrating to wholesale inattention, once announced to her planeload of commuters, "If the oxygen mask falls, just place it over your navel and continue breathing normally." Nobody even looked up at her.

Ironically, the only people on the plane liable to be carefully reading the briefing card are experts—pilots, engineers—who know that the configuration of various airplane models differs, and they have a normal human curiosity about where the exits happen to be on a given flight. And I've heard at least one say he reads the card hoping that will encourage other people on the plane to do it, too.

Sometimes, as I pore over the card, the person sitting next to me will smile indulgently at me as if I were a country bumpkin who's never been on one of them-there aeroplanes before. What I, a spineless coward who craves approval from total strangers, usually say is "Oh, I'm sort of an information freak." What a normal, well-adjusted, informed person would say is "You don't read the card?" accompanied by a pitying glance meant to convey, "You poor schmo, now I'll probably have to save *your* life, too."

2. Count the seats between you and the nearest exit, and an alternative. Just do it. I don't want to lie awake nights thinking, "Oh, I forgot to tell them how to find the exit if there's smoke."

3. This is the brace position: put your crossed arms against the seat in front of you, rest your head on your arms, and put your feet as far forward as possible. Many times the survivors of crashes have been people who knew, and got into, the brace position. The traditional advice is "Grab your ankles," but have you ever tried to *see* your ankles, much less grab them, in a crowded airliner? The position I described above is the one generally recommended by the FAA. When in doubt, grab your ankles. And in *any* case, do it exactly as the flight attendant tells you to do it.

4. If there is an emergency, act *fast*. Reading the studies, I get the impression the main problem for most accident survivors seems to have been getting out of their seats. Sometimes another person had to yell at

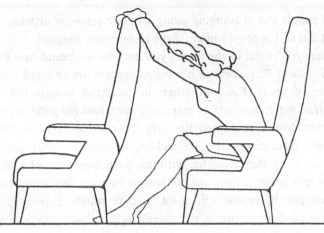

them to *move*. You may have to yell at yourself. If the flight attendant is telling you what to do, that's great, he or she has practiced this drill over and over. Flight attendants have a curious job—the part of the job they're most intensively trained to do is the part they usually go their entire careers without doing while they're on the job.

But they might be very busy, so start without them. Don't wait around to be instructed. A recent experiment suggested that most people would not use the oxygen masks unless someone specifically ordered them to. I hereby order you to use the oxygen mask if it falls.

And you're probably going to have to *pull* on it, which you will know how to do if you listen to the briefing, but whatever you're worrying about at the time, don't worry about breaking an oxygen mask. A representative of an oxygen mask manufacturer told me about a Pakistani flight which had a pressurization problem, and the masks fell—above the passengers' heads because the passengers were supposed to pull the masks *down* to operate them. But the passengers politely *stood up* to the masks' level. "And then," he said, "they all sat back down." Rather suddenly, and woozily, because no oxygen was coming out of the masks. Don't worry, they all landed all right, but they should have listened to the safety briefing.

4. I would've thought it was obvious that now is not the time to be worrying about heroically rescuing your overnight bag, but I am told one of the flight attendants' biggest headaches during an evacuation is

arguing people out of bringing along all their carry-on articles. Please. Just get *out* of the stupid plane. Live to buy new luggage.

5. Once you're out of the plane, you may have a brand-new problem —water. About 70 percent of all major airports are situated right next to bodies of water. Even so, what the technical experts like to call "unplanned water contact" is extremely rare, and life jackets generally just gather dust. *But,* pay particularly close attention when the flight attendant demonstrates the life jackets, because I gather few of the experts are altogether delighted with this particular piece of equipment. It seems that some airlines use life jackets that are too complicated for easy operation by people with a lot on their minds. Especially people who have paid no attention whatsoever when that operation was explained to them.

Now I have a question for you. Have I created a monster?

I really hate to think about you out there somewhere, gentle reader, spring-loaded for disaster, flinging yourself into brace position at every engine sputter, leaping to your feet and yelling, "Everybody out! Follow me!" if there's a rough landing. People have been known to hurt themselves overreacting to what they *thought* was an emergency situation. In early 1986, a flame shot out of an engine on a jet taxiing up to take off from Kennedy Airport. While that doesn't happen too frequently, it's merely a result of fuel residue being burned off and does *not* constitute an emergency, but somebody onboard didn't know that, and activated the emergency chutes. About twenty-five passengers slid onto the runway in a panic, ignoring the crew's efforts to stop them, and fifteen of them were hurt, one seriously, in the completely unnecessary confusion.

And my heart goes out to a woman described in Dr. Johnson's book. It seems the fire department at a large airport had been alerted of a possible emergency landing. As they waited on the runway, they saw a 747 landing, and a flame briefly belched out of one engine, so they assumed *this* was the emergency, and the 747 pilot was radioed that his plane was on fire. Which it was not, but naturally he ordered an evacuation. Actually, the plane with the emergency was landing on another runway. When the pilot found out, he sent a crew member to try to stop the evacuation. The crew member found people sitting frozen on the plane when for all they knew they should have been getting out as quickly as possible. One woman was lying in the aisle in what was described as a "rigid, trance-like state."

I can relate. I've flown in a rigid, trance-like state when the only mention of exits I heard the entire flight was during the safety briefing.

Sometimes untoward incidents happen on a plane which will only threaten your life if you let them scare the daylights out of you. If the oxygen masks do pop out, for instance, it is probably due to any one of a number of nondeadly reasons, which is a nice thing to know, even though it's been estimated that oxygen masks are "deployed" about once every 740,000 flight hours (so that record-breaking old DC-3 we talked about earlier still has about seventy-four flight years to go before it can expect its first oxygen mask deployment). An aborted takeoff run, an engine that has to be shut down in flight, a pressurization problem, even a quick burst of flame out an engine are each unusual, and each taken very seriously by the airlines and the authorities, who will analyze them scrupulously, but in none of these cases would a frantic scramble for the emergency exits be in order. Go ahead and ask the flight attendant, "Excuse me, but what the hell was *that?*" And after you land, if the incident has been very dramatic, you may want to call the FAA hot line (1-800-FAA-SURE) and tell them something very dramatic happened on your flight and you want to know why. They'll check it out, write you, and tell you what they found out.

At least, they promised me this is the way they handle the hot line.

If the situation were more serious than that, I don't think you'd be needing me to provide you with any Tips on How to Tell If Your Plane Has Crashed. You would be, however, probably the best prepared non-crew-member on the entire plane.

Chances are you'll fly monotonously all the traveling days of your life —just look at all the retired pilots and flight attendants in the world who flew on most of the days of their long careers, and all the frequent fliers who practically consider airliners to be their offices. I read a newspaper article recently written by a famous columnist who was complaining about efforts by safety officials to limit the amount of carry-on luggage. The safety people are worried about stuff falling out and hitting passengers on the head, but the columnist said he flies four to five hours every *day* and has never seen anyone hit on the head. I don't think he has the proper attitude toward aviation safety, but he's reportedly a good friend of President Reagan's so I expect he'll be all right.

Now that you know what to do in cases that will *never* happen, perhaps we should turn our attention to handling an emergency we can be pretty sure *will* happen. You've probably faced this emergency many times. You may, in fact, be even more terrified of this particular emergency than of any other. When fearful fliers in classes are asked, "What is the worst thing that could happen on your next flight?" many do not say, "The plane will crash" or "I'll get killed." A surprising number say something like "I'll lose control" or "I'll start screaming" or "I'll get so scared I'll pass out."

This is the worst fear of all. Fear of yourself. But you are in luck. Of all the events going on in and around your plane—mechanical, natural, human—that will affect your comfort on your next flight, there's only one over which you have active, direct control: what's going on in your mind.

Getting Through

HIGH FLIGHT

Oh, I have slipped the surly bonds of earth
And danced the skies on laughter-silvered wings;
Sunward I've climbed and joined the tumbling mirth
Of sun-split clouds—and done a hundred things
You have not dreamed of—wheeled and soared and swung
High in the sunlit silence. Hov'ring there,
I've chased the shouting winds along and flung
My eager craft through footless halls of air.
Up, up the long delirious burning blue
I've topped the wind-swept heights with easy grace,
Where never lark, or even eagle, flew;
And, while with silent, lifting mind I've trod
The high untrespassed sanctity of space,
Put out my hand, and touched the face of God.

John Gillespie Magee, Jr.

That is probably the most famous, most frequently quoted poem ever written about flying. Graduates of fearful fliers' courses are often given a framed copy as a diploma. I certainly don't want you to be deprived just because you got your course out of a book.

But that is probably also the most beautiful, most nearly perfect description you ever heard of how you do *not* feel about flying.

For years I've had the wrong idea about "High Flight." I used to hear it all the time, usually at the end of the broadcasting day on a local TV station, right before the national anthem, accompanied by stirring trumpets and radiant views of cloudbanks shot with sun. I figured it came from the flowing pen of the same school of poets with three names who write those inspirational books with titles like *Life's Golden Paths* that great-aunts like to give for wedding presents. I was fairly sure that if a plane I was on commenced any wheeling, swinging, or flinging, I would not be tumbling with mirth. I'm still sure.

I can go along with Mr. Magee on one point. Earth can be pretty surly, all right. Compared to what a normal twentieth-century adult risks every ordinary day, not only bodily harm from a thousand sources, but humiliation, loss, failure, heartbreak, and assorted nasty surprises, we should probably think of an airline flight as a brief time-out, some time in a safe place. Our white knuckles should probably start when we *land*.

Down here on the ground, though, the risks, the scariness, are sort of diffused. Yes, you're afraid of spiders, so you run away from them or squish them with your shoe. Yes, heart disease is a major killer. Maybe you'll stop smoking and start running, if not tomorrow, next week at the latest. There've been some break-ins in the neighborhood, better get new locks next time you're at the hardware store. Boy, it's getting to where you take your life in your *hands* on the freeway these days, you drove by a bad wreck last week, really should start wearing your seat belt.

Flying is different. There the fear is nicely concentrated. When your plane starts hurtling down the runway at 150 m.p.h., and you go precariously (so it feels) clambering into the air, that big, nebulous future where we put most of our fears in storage suddenly gets very, very small.

If you are mortally afraid of a plane crash, the simple, overriding reality seems to be that you are, at that moment, on a plane. You know that the possibility of trouble should be extremely remote. You also know that the possibility is now sitting in your *lap*, and will be vividly, inescapably sitting there for the length of the flight. If Something Happens, it won't be someday, it will be within the next hour, or two hours, or whatever that fixed, specific, absolutely immediate time is. You can't get off. You can't get around it.

You can get through it, though. And I'm not talking about simply *enduring* another monster chiller horror flight. You already know how to do that. I am talking about *one flight* with less fear, more control, and a changed perspective. It's not true that once you take off you can't change your mind. Changing the mind you bring aboard your next flight is the whole trick.

You will find in this chapter a selection of simple techniques, some for use before the flight, to help prevent the worst of the fear before it ever gets started, and some for during the flight, to deal effectively with that immediate, flash-fire panic we all know and loathe.

One flight with a changed mind may be all you need to put that vivid possibility of trouble where it belongs: so astronomically distant from any given flight that it is a tiny pinpoint in the vast constellation of possibilities. It certainly doesn't need to be sitting in your *lap*.

For now, we aren't going to worry about all the rest of the flights you will or will not take the rest of your life. We aren't going to try to ascertain whether or not you are "over" your fear of flying. My definition of getting over a fear is arriving somehow at a point where it no longer has any power over you at all, where all that's left is an occasional mild apprehension, maybe (like when you read the paper). No trace, anyway, of what used to be a blazing terror. I do not doubt that someday you will be flying along and you will realize, probably with some surprise, that you are, indeed, *over* your fear of flying. Might even be on your very next flight.

Well, it's *conceivable,* but I would be as surprised as you. More likely, you still have a few things to figure out before that semi-miraculous transformation occurs. You should fully expect to feel some level of fear the next time you're up in a plane. But, with a little preparation, you can also expect real, positive changes in the way you experience flight. Getting over is a question of time and thought and perception, a process probably every bit as complicated as the reasons you came down with the fear in the first place. Getting through is just a question of management.

So book the flight. Even if your present feelings run more along the

lines of: "Oh, I have been dragged kicking and screaming from earth/
And dueled with death on panic-stricken wings."

BEFORE THE FLIGHT

1. Even if you've flown a hundred and fifty horrible times, let's start
all over and count the *next* one as a brand-new experience. Try to
arrange to take your "maiden flight" just for the flight's sake—not for
business, or even for a vacation. The importance of this varies with the
severity of your fear. If you have been very afraid of flying for a long
time, the best way to start flying is to take a short flight to a destination
not associated with any pressure or significance of its own. Just pick a
spot about an hour's flight from your local airport, fly there some pleasant afternoon when nothing else is worrying you, congratulate yourself
on how well you did, and fly back.

The lead time you should allow yourself to get your mind right for
this occasion also depends on you. Some classes take eight or even
twenty weeks to work up to an actual flight. Some go from orientation
to graduation in three days. What you want to beware of, however, is
assigning your flight to Sometime in the Future If I Don't Die Some
Other Way First. A month or so should give you plenty of time to
practice whatever in this chapter you decide to practice, and take advantage of the cheapest fares, too. And at that point, you're probably
going to be as ready as you'll ever be for the most important practice of
all—the kind you can only get by flying.

Actually making a reservation, so that you have a specific day to
work toward, is the indispensable first step. You have to promise yourself that on such-and-such a day, you're *going* to fly, no matter if your
sinuses are acting up or the weather is crummy or your horoscope
warns against travel—no matter what. Once you get the basic decision
out of the way, you can concentrate on *how* you're going to fly, not if or
when.

If a special "orientation" flight isn't practical for you, don't worry.
The whole point of reading this book may have been to prepare yourself
to fly to your next convention in Hawaii, in which case there are more
than enough psychological devices in this chapter to get you comfortably there and back.

But if at all possible, at least schedule your next flight for a time when you're not overly tired or pressured. A tall order, I know. The last time I was neither tired nor pressured was sometime during seventh grade. However, psychologists agree that fatigue can dramatically lower your resistance to situational stress.

On a red-eye flight from Chicago to Washington one predawn, after a somewhat festive night that included most activities except sleep, I came within the merest hairsbreadth of running up the aisle and beating on the door and begging to be let out before we took off. I didn't just suspect we were going to crash; I KNEW. I could see the aftermath with Jeanne Dixon clarity. I knew the exact words my mother would say on being told. My seat was next to a congressman, and I knew my death would be the tiniest footnote to his. I stood in the bathroom and wept over my wasted, footnote life. Controlled hysteria in flight had always been my standard M.O. That flight was different. I went, in a word, crazy. Believe me, you are going to feel very silly if you do this. Get some rest.

2. When you make your reservations, ask for an aisle seat next to an exit. If you have an aisle seat, you can get up as often as you like without mumbling polite, made-up excuses, and you will probably feel less confined. If you are sitting near an exit, you'll be one of the first out even if they somehow manage to crash the plane.

Choosing your seat and having your reasons is a good way to start getting control over the circumstances of your flight.

A former pilot, who now works for ALPA and spends a great deal of time on planes, told me he always asks for a seat next to the exit. So you can escape, I said. No, because there's more leg room, he said.

So if you would like to give the reservationist the impression that you are an extremely savvy and experienced flier and actually *using* the exit is the farthest thing from your mind, you might casually say, "Oh, and could you get me a seat next to an exit, there's always so much more *leg room* there."

Perhaps someday I will write a book helping people get over their fear of embarrassing themselves in front of total strangers (guess I'll have to get over it myself first).

After one or two flights in this training seat, you probably won't care any more where you sit.

3. Most behavior modification-type phobia treatments, including the major fearful fliers' courses, work at least in part on the principle of desensitization, which is a fine technical term for getting used to what scares you so it doesn't scare you any more. Basically, desensitization involves going through—either in real life or in your imagination— various stages of a frightening activity, step-by-step, working your way up gradually from the least bothersome to the most blood-curdling. This progression is usually performed in conjunction with a deep relaxation technique, so that you are in effect teaching your body to react to each stage with pleasant sensations of calm instead of fear and loathing.

With a phobia like, say, ailurophobia (fear of cats), such a treatment is fairly straightforward: a person might start with pictures of cats, move gradually on to stuffed cats, then to just looking at a real cat, and finally to holding one. Don't snicker, there are lots of nice people for whom touching a cat is even more profoundly horrifying than riding in an airliner is for you.

With fear of flying, you can see how a complete course of on-the-spot desensitization is a little more problematical. You can probably arrange dress rehearsals of driving to the airport, standing in the ticket line, going up to the gate, even perhaps sitting on a parked plane, and if you are truly, deeply terrified even of those preliminaries, you should consider doing so. But unless you hire your own plane and pilot, the really scary parts of an airline flight are hard to do in easy stages. You can't do a takeoff and say, "Okay, that's enough for today, tomorrow I'll try to get through cruising."

You are going to have to use your imagination. In this case, that's probably an advantage. If you can desensitize yourself to the dreadful conditions *you* imagine, an actual plane ride will be mild in comparison. Sort of like an ailurophobe desensitizing himself with live leopards.

Instead of spending part of every day before the flight as if it were countdown to Armageddon, you can spend part of every day doing a little amateur desensitization: sitting quietly by yourself, with your eyes closed, relaxing deeply as you visualize each step in the flight. You can do it in your lawn chair if you promise not to get ideas.

For this process you need two tools: a "hierarchy," or list of the various components of the flight (for example, sitting in the gate area, walking to the plane, buckling yourself in, and so on), from the least anxious moments right through to the scariest thing you can imagine happening; and a deep relaxation method. I have supplied you, beginning on page 125, with both.

Decide in advance some way to measure each level of fear, each little stairstep on the staircase to Maximum Fright Flight Overload. You can do this fear-o-meter any way you like; some people try to imagine exactly how many wild horses it would take to drag them through some phase of the flight or other. I have used a rather pedestrian straight numbering system—1 for "I'm perfectly serene, this doesn't bother me a bit" through to 10 for "My hair is going white at the roots." You'll start out by relaxing and imagining the easy little 2s and 3s. Making the reservation, for instance. And work up through the midranges of checking in and waiting at the gate. And then, when you're getting to be an old hand at relaxing yourself, you'll tackle all the 8-through-10s (which may, of course, be every single second from the first move the plane makes once you're on it).

The hierarchy I've provided (in Appendix I) is only an example. It's the progression *I* found scariest, but you have to figure out exactly what scares *you*, and thus what you should be practicing, and you have to come up with the corresponding mental images. You may not be the least disturbed until the plane actually takes off. There are a surprising number of people who can handle takeoff just fine if they can just get through the *airport*—the crowds, the smell, and the high ceilings scare the daylights out of them. And some people get panicky even looking at a *picture* of an airplane. If you're one of these, you'd better get started, you've got a lot of desensitizing to do.*

But wherever you *start* your hierarchy, probably the most important part is imagining the worst that could happen. I haven't supplied an example of that. I don't want to chance describing something awful you've never thought of before, but you know what that most horrible conceivable eventuality is. I know you can't stand even *thinking* about it. In fact, you have probably spent hours on planes struggling mightily to keep that very thought out of your mind. Well, buck up. This may be the hardest thing you have to do to get over your fear of flying—harder,

---

* But if you are one of these, you're clearly an example of human psychical evolution at its peak, since your nervous system is honed to overreact even to *symbols*, and no doubt you are brilliant enough to overcome anything.

for some, than flying itself—but it's also one of the most useful. So work up to it, get as relaxed as possible, go someplace where you feel safe—go sit in a hospital emergency room waiting area if you think you might scare yourself into a heart attack—and get it over with. Conjure and deal with the image on the ground, and it will have less power over you in the air.

Now, the relaxation method. Deep relaxation has become so trendy that if you've read a newspaper or a magazine in the last ten years you've probably seen more than one technique, but I'll give you an easy one. If you actually practice the routine every day for a few weeks, you'll find that it comes in handy for all sorts of stressful situations. You'll be using it for occasions such as entertaining your in-laws long after you've stopped needing it to fly.

In fact, some experts believe that the relaxation part of desensitization is not as important as the simple continued *exposure* to the object of fear, even if the exposure is only imagined. In some experiments, people with various phobias improved just as much when they were exposed numerous times to the source of their fear *without* any special relaxation exercises. By this principle, the more you fly, the less afraid you'll get, even if you take no other measures.

But as you have no doubt noticed if you've been flying for years and getting progressively *more* terrified, exposure works both ways. Practice makes perfect, whether you're practicing being frightened or being calm. If you've been using every flight to polish your panic drill, you might be very good at it by now. Hereafter, you are going to practice tranquility instead.

There isn't anything magic about the precise order of the hierarchy or the exact synchronization of relaxation and mental image or any other single element. Phobia research is a fairly hot area, right now, and believe me, folks, they've tried everything—desensitization with hierarchies and without, with relaxation and without, exposure with reinforcement and without, and a great many other permutations withal. To date, most combinations work on somebody and no combination works on everybody.

What is important for you is the process of *thinking through* what scares you (composing a hierarchy is usually a very enlightening exercise on this point) and *changing your physical reactions* (learning to relax on command gives your body a viable option to full-scramble red alert).

4. Go to an airport and watch at least twenty planes take off, and watch at least twenty land. Go by yourself. Go when you have no other errand at the airport: not when you're picking someone up, and *not* on a day when you're flying yourself.

If you don't do anything else in this chapter, go to an airport and watch planes take off and land. There is no easier, surer way to connect your internal experience of flight to an external reality.

It isn't always easy to find a good vantage point. I walked all over National Airport in Washington, D.C., several different times, going through security at every turn, trying to look cool when I disobeyed signs that said PASSENGERS ONLY, checking out the view at every gate in the whole place. You can see almost anything at that airport except planes. Your airport, too, may give you the impression that you are on a fool's errand, but persevere.

Airliners close up look, at least to me, sort of beat-up and altogether improbable. A pack of airliners in line to take off doesn't give an impression of power, grace, highness, or mightiness, but rather of one more traffic problem in a world of traffic problems. When the lead plane gets the signal to go, and begins to gather speed, it looks to me like somebody's idea of a joke, as if you and I decided we could get a mobile home airborne if we could just get it rolling fast enough. I think a plane's first few moments off the ground look almost as untenable from the ground as they feel from inside.

Once an airliner is airborne, though, I can sort of see John Gillespie Magee's point. The craft almost *does* look eager—eager to get up into its element. I have no idea if you will have the same impression, but that doesn't matter. The important thing is to fix in your mind a clear, concrete image of planes in action, planes that have nothing whatsoever to do with you.

While you're at it, go ahead and imagine that a few of the horrible things you're afraid of when *you* are aboard are actually happening to the planes you are watching. Don't worry, what those people don't know won't hurt them. Confirm to yourself once and for all that no matter how powerfully you imagine a plane disintegrating, flopping over, bursting into flames, whatever you can cook up, those dastardly thoughts don't affect it one bit, any more than you could mentally levitate your blender. The plane sails heedlessly on. (If you *can* bring a plane down by psychic projection, you might want to check in with the CIA. Please don't tell them where you got the idea.)

5. Just for the sake of argument, let's assume that your next flight will be like the other sixteen thousand or so on the same day every day and nothing will occur to physically threaten your life. So, if you get scared, we can assume that the trigger will be a thought as opposed to an external reality. Logically, therefore, what you need most is a way to control your thoughts.

Contriving a really effective way of doing this is the dream of psychologists (and nuns) everywhere. About the best they (the psychologists) have come up with are two methods called "thought-stopping" and "thought-switching."

As you go through your desensitizing, of course, you'll be deliberately summoning a great many frightening thoughts. But you certainly don't want to be at their mercy *all the time.* Set aside that one, small daily period for lining up and dealing with your scary visions. Declare the rest of your days and nights off-limits.

Thought-stopping means exactly what it says: each and every time you catch yourself worrying about your upcoming flight, *instantly* command yourself to "STOP!" in the loudest and most peremptory mental voice you can summon. An accompanying mental image will help—crashing cymbals, for instance, or an enormous red stop sign, or a steel door clanging down.

Then immediately take a deep breath, make a conscious effort to relax, and focus your mind on whatever is around you at that moment. If you're at the office, for instance, get *very* interested in what's on your desk, as if you were shortly going to have to give an inventory of it from memory. As you lie in your bed at 3 A.M., on the other hand, there might not be much to look at (no offense), so you might try something like remembering in detail every date you've ever been on in your life. The "STOP!" must be compelling enough to break up the thought at least for a few seconds, and you really have to practice this pretty relentlessly until the sequence of thought-STOP-relax-focus becomes nearly automatic.

Like most normal fearful fliers, you probably do a lot of talking to yourself before a flight, beginning as soon as the trip is decided ("Oh, God, this means I'll have to fly, I *hate* to fly, this is going to be terrible") and continuing in the same vein ("When that thing starts taking off I'm going to be petrified, I'm always petrified, and what if there's turbulence, there's bound to be turbulence, I bet we hit a really big air pocket, if we hit an air pocket I'm going to faint") and so on. In effect, you are carefully rehearsing yourself for how miserable you plan to be. Thought-switching is a way to give yourself new instructions.

As soon as you notice you are once again reminding yourself in detail how much you are going to hate some aspect of the flight, immediately STOP, relax, and focus on an alternative idea. For example, instead of "I'll probably start getting scared right when we take off," consciously substitute "When we take off, I'll probably start getting scared, but I'll be able to relax and after a few minutes it won't be so bad."

Now, you must take care, in this process, to emphasize the aspects of the flight that you can control. When you think, "The plane is going to crash," you don't substitute "No, it isn't" or you're liable to get into a perfectly useless knock-down-drag-out argument with yourself.

"The plane is going to crash."

"No, it isn't."

"Oh, yeah? Well, I say it is."

"No, you idiot, it's one in three million."

"Well, *you're* one in three million."

"I know, but I'm not the *only* one in three million."

And so on until if you had four arms you would come to blows, and the little sourpuss is going to have the last word, anyway, by saying, "Well, it *might.*"

Don't worry about what will happen. Worry about what you're going to do. Your substitute thought should tend toward "I'm going to *feel* as if the plane is about to crash, but as soon as I do, I'll start relaxing and in about five minutes I'll feel much more in control."

The key to using either thought-stopping or thought-switching is to exercise, firmly and repeatedly, at least some control over *every* thought you have about flying. If both processes remind you of housebreaking a puppy, it's because the principle is similar. You have to notice immediately, catch yourself in the act, and whisk yourself outside.

6. Spend a little time going over the part of this book that describes

normal flight procedure (see Chapter 2). Know in advance that there
are bound to be variations. The pilot and plane respond to the conditions of each flight, which vary with the kind of plane, the route, the
weather, the winds, the airport, the weight the plane is carrying, the
traffic in the area, and so forth.

Generally, though, you want to be prepared for how the flight is
likely to feel and sound. If you know what the sounds mean (and now
you do), and the same sounds keep happening, after a while you'll look
for new sounds, and since commercial aviation is so tediously uneventful, you won't hear many, and your mind, bored, will start torturing
you with something else.

I'm not going to suggest that you take the book onboard and follow
along. If you're embarrassed over the phone with a reservationist, you
probably will *really* try to be cool in front of the other passengers.
Perhaps you could switch the cover of this book with that of *Putting the
Artistry Back in Sex* or *Investing Your Second Million.* Then something
might happen to completely take your mind off your troubles.

But you might want to use as a bookmark one small discreet index
card, with a few notations of any facts or strategies you particularly
want to remember. Sometimes on that first flight a person might get a
little nervous, and momentarily forget every single helpful hint he or
she has ever read. A glance at your—I mean his or her—cheat sheet can
quicky restore him or her to the business at hand.

7. If there are any little rituals you would like to perform, go ahead
and perform them, you don't have to go cold turkey right away. There's
no sense getting up in the air and thinking: "If only I had told Horace I
love him." Clean the house if you want to, or leave a mess if you think
that would be luckier. Buy $300,000 worth of insurance for a dollar in
the airport if it comforts you (don't tell your beneficiaries if you think
they might be so comforted your feelings would be hurt). Don't breathe
a word to anyone that you're in the process of getting unafraid of flying,
if you think that would be unlucky. Pack your rabbit's feet, cross your
fingers, cross yourself, wear your lucky charm, smoke 'em if you got
'em, use voodoo, necromancy, animal sacrifice, good deeds, whatever
psychological or metaphysical armament you feel as if you still need.

DURING THE FLIGHT

1. If, as you board, you introduce yourself to the flight attendant or the pilot, and tell them that you are nervous about flying, I can just about guarantee you that they will be very gracious. The pilot will probably make announcements during the flight that he or she wouldn't ordinarily make, explaining procedures as he or she goes, and the flight attendants will give you as much extra, reassuring attention as they have time for. Most fearful fliers watch the flight attendants' eyes all during the flight, anyway, looking for that flicker of doubt that means something is amiss. You might as well tell them why you're going to be staring at them. I once saw a flight attendant charging down the aisle looking so distressed I was sure we were all goners, but it turned out somebody was trying to pay for a beer with a $50 bill.

You can usually count on the crew's discretion, too. In other words, the pilot is not likely to announce, "Now let's all give the man in 28B a great big hand for finally getting the guts to fly."

I would not have done what I have just told you to do in a million years, a character flaw which I admit only because you, too, may think you're too shy or, as in my case, too vain to reveal your dark secret to the professionals in charge. But the airline people encourage it, and pilots tell me they enjoy it.

I'm told most of the passengers who come up before a flight to look around the cockpit usually bring one of their children as a front. "Timmy's REALLY interested in airplanes," they'll say, while Timmy dozes in the doorway and the adult who commandeered him asks to try out the throttle. Experts like SOAR's Captain Tom Bunn practically *insist* that every fearful flier should begin his or her flight by meeting the pilot, however briefly. Really, all you have to do is pop your head into the cockpit, and say, "Watch those bumps if you can, I'm not too crazy about flying." On this first flight, you should try *everything*, even if you have to borrow someone's kid.

2. Now remember you have to pay attention to the safety briefing. Your nerves are probably already going to be nudging you a little at this point, but you simply must say, "Nerves, time out, I have to listen to this, I'll be with you in a minute and we can resume being terrified."

Just take time to listen, read the card, scout the exits, and count the intervening seats. You will then have taken care of all possible external emergency contingencies and can focus on your interior alarms.

3. The first few minutes are probably going to be the hardest. For a large percentage of fearful fliers, takeoff is the most spine-tingling time. Not only is takeoff the best symbolic juncture for a really juicy existential panic, but the engines change pitch and rhythm a few times, usually because of noise abatement procedures, and climbing through the cloud cover can be the bumpiest part of the ride. The plane might also begin a pretty dramatic banking turn almost right away.

Here's what you do:

Count slowly to three hundred—one thousand one, one thousand two—beginning with the instant the wheels leave the ground. Keep counting. I don't care if both wings peel off, I don't care if the roof splits in two or the plane twirls in the air like Rita Mae's baton. No matter what appalling thing seems to be happening, *keep counting*. Give what you are positive is an untoward development at least three hundred full seconds before you scream for the flight attendant.

About 30 percent of all accidents occur in the first five minutes or so after takeoff. If anything's *ever* going to happen, it's probably going to happen while you're counting. That means, first, that you will have a nice clear head to deal with any possible emergency, and, second, when you finish counting you'll be out of the danger zone and you don't have to worry again until right before landing.

While you're counting, try to notice exactly where you're clenched (you are bound to be clenched somewhere). Likely candidates: your fingers, your face, your ankles, and the muscles around your—um, posterior. Relax each. You can't hold a 727 up with any of them.

I still count the seconds during takeoff, out of habit. The difference is, I used to get to three hundred and start over again. Now I hardly ever get past twenty without forgetting all about it.

Two other things to remember during takeoff: how the planes you watched at the airport took off, one after another, without a hitch, doing just exactly what your plane is doing now; and the Bernoulli effect—the pressure under the wings is greater than the pressure above them. Your plane isn't precariously levitating off the ground. Your plane is being forced implacably, mechanically into the air.

4. You're at three hundred. You know how I've been telling you that you are going to be scared? Right about now is when you can expect a strong surge of oh-NOW-I-remember-what-was-so-horrible.

There is an old story about a boy who was terrified of kreplach. Kreplach is a sort of kosher dumpling. The little boy couldn't be in the same *room* with it, much less eat it. I guess the family ate a lot of kreplach, so this screaming and crying got to be so worrisome that the family doctor was consulted. He'd never heard of anybody who was afraid of kreplach, but the doctor was sure the child's terror could be alleviated if the mother would just patiently show him each ingredient and explain the cooking process step-by-step. So his mother set out to cure her son of this nonsensical fear by sitting him down to watch her make kreplach. She carefully explained every step in a soothing motherly voice. "Now, here's the meat, darling, I'm chopping it up, is the meat scary?" "No, Mama, it's just meat." "Of course it is, precious, now here's the dough, I'm going to take a little bit of dough and make a square, now is there anything scary about dough?" "Dough? Oh, Mama, come *on.*" "You're doing so well, dear. And now I'm going to put this meat into this dough and just tuck in the edges, nothing scary about that, hmmm?" The boy shook his head, watching calmly until the last edge was tucked, at which point his eyes grew very wide. "Eeek! Kreplach!" he screamed, and fled the kitchen.

And it may be that you have been nodding calmly at all the wonderful statistics, all the parts and structures which cannot fail, all the painstaking procedures and the monumental safeguards, and you've been reasonably convinced—until this moment, when they all suddenly disappear, and all you can see is the dreaded kreplach. You're *flying.*

You now have a choice. You can give up, tell yourself you *knew* none of that psychological mumbo-jumbo would work, get a viselike grip on the armrests, and huddle miserably in your seat for the rest of the flight, composing a nasty letter to my publisher. That's what you'll probably want to do. Or you can figure you're stuck up there anyway, you might as well do a few of the things you practiced and compose the letter when you land.

If you have the presence of mind to decide the latter, you're about 95 percent of the way to being over your fear of flying.

So, assuming you're not going to flee the kitchen, begin by deciding just how afraid you are, on the scale you used for your hierarchy. Let's say you listen to yourself squealing for a few seconds and decide you are just about, but not quite, as scared as you can possibly be—a 9, say. All right.

Stop. Shake your head. Call up that commanding STOP image.

Relax. Take three *slow* deep breaths. Unclench those problem areas again.

Focus. Look very closely at the weave of the fabric on the seat in front of you. Count the buttons on your shirt. Pick a face a few rows ahead and examine it as if you were going to have to describe it to a police artist.

Announce to yourself that, just as you expected, you now have the feeling the plane is going to crash, so, just as you planned, you are now going to go through your relaxation exercise, with the objective of reducing your 9 to a 7.

And keep in mind that once adrenaline is released, it takes a few minutes to subside, no matter what you do, so expect that these announcements to yourself will be accompanied by sweaty palms and a racing motor in your chest. But most of all, remember that just because you're going from a 5 to a 10 doesn't mean the flight is getting doubly dangerous. I used to consult my *fear* to determine whether or not the plane was in trouble. The bigger my fear was, the more trouble I figured the plane was in. This is sort of like trying to gauge the weather outside by how loud your alarm clock sounds. Hmmm, sounds really loud this morning, must be a tornado bearing down on my house.

Number one, your adrenaline is not an aviation expert. Number two, the plane is paying no attention whatsoever to your mental processes. Airplanes have surprisingly little emotional sensitivity.

5. Now is the time to do your relaxation exercise with a vengeance. Well, try to do it a little less grimly than that. Remember, if you can somehow get your muscles to relax, you are not going to register fear. I am not making this up. This is a proven fact. Generations of laboratory animals, not to mention psychology majors, have given their lives to establish this. Your brain may be sending out the same old alarms, but if you can get your muscles to relax, your brain will be playing to empty seats.

So wiggle your toes and get started. If by the time you get up to your stomach you find yourself thinking about mowing the lawn or firing your secretary or something, remind yourself sternly that you are supposed to be terrified, and start again. You're already cured but you don't want all that practice to go to waste.

Throughout the flight, keep monitoring your fear, even to the point of noting down the number at various stages on your little index card, or on the in-fright—sorry, Freudian typo, make that in-flight—magazine. After you land, if you have made any changes at all, from a 9 to a 7 and then to a 6, for example, you have a good excuse for self-congratulation. As you do if you come away with a line of perfect 10s, just for *surviving*.

6. Look out the window. Not only is everything likely to be gorgeous out there, but focusing on the horizon or some other point in the far distance is often recommended as a good way to head off approaching nausea and/or panic. Turning the air up full blast and pointing the stream at your face will also help.

Incidentally, if you have never flown before and are afraid of getting airsick, don't be. Even in the fifties, when planes flew much lower and much less smoothly, it's been estimated that only one half of 1 percent of airline passengers got airsick. They must have made a real mess, however, because they had a far-reaching effect. Little paper airsickness bags are still dutifully packed in every seat pocket on virtually every commercial flight. You're liable to get queasier contemplating a bag expressly designed to throw up into than you will by the motions of the plane, which are nothing like the regular, rolling motions of a boat. One senior flight attendant who has flown for fifteen years told me she could only remember one adult (a pregnant lady) and several excited little kids ever making use of the airsickness equipment.

Not much in the pressurized, carefully regulated atmosphere of a modern airliner should cause you to get sick (although it will dry out your skin something fierce) unless you have a cold or sinus condition. In that case, taking off and cruising won't bother you, but landing might be downright painful. Descending from high altitudes can aggravate pressure in your inner ears. Generally, taking a decongestant and yawning and swallowing hard a lot will take the pressure off. Anyway, fear of earaches is an entirely different phobia. Talk to your doctor.

7. You cannot expect an imagination as lively and creative as yours to

just roll over and go to sleep, no matter how relaxed you get. Perhaps you can exercise your talents in a somewhat different way.

I was surprised to find there is actually a name for the idea I'm about to describe, which I'd always thought was entirely a product of my own weird imagination. Psychologists call a similar version the "blow-up" technique, but I'm not going to try to pass the following off as science. All I can say is it occurred to me out of desperation, and it worked for me, but I believe its appeal is limited to a certain kind of very strange mind.

During one bad (for me) flight, I noticed that I had become deeply engrossed in the idea that the engines did not sound right. I was staring at the wing, imagining in detail how in a few minutes I'd hear a rattle, then a clunk, then I'd see black smoke and fan blades tearing through the cowling, then . . . I was suddenly struck with how *real* this imaginary scenario seemed, might as well have been in Technicolor. I thought, boy, I bet I could imagine the hell out of anything, I'm going to try to imagine something really *spectacular.* What I decided to imagine was the cockpit door opening, and the pilot stepping out, dressed in a black cocktail gown. "Ladies and gentlemen," he said, "please don't be alarmed, but I can't take this charade any longer, I'm a woman trapped in the body of a man." I spent the better part of a flight from Dallas to Denver following these dramatic developments (see, his wife happened to be on the flight, too, and his revelation came as a complete surprise to her, and her first thought was for their five children and . . .), but we landed before I could finish so I don't know how the story turned out.

Since then, every time I catch myself in a vivid reverie about Trouble Aloft, I immediately substitute the most ludicrous, most farfetched imaginary extravaganza I can possibly come up with—Bengal tigers escaped from the cargo section, aphrodisiacs slipped into everyone's peanuts—okay, I'll spare you any more lurid personal examples, including the one about Elvis Presley's ghost which absorbed me all the way from Los Angeles to Honolulu, but you get the picture. The idea must be preposterous, involved, and graphic. You must concentrate. I don't know about you, but for me, timidly imagining that the plane is going to land and I'm going to live out my life won't do the trick. The point is not just to amuse yourself (although, on a plane, if you don't, who will) but rather to remind yourself that *all* these pictures—the ones you think are "realistic," the ones you know are utterly outrageous—are coming from the same powerful place: your own imagination.

Events are limited. Imagination is boundless.

8. Now, about having that third or fourth drink. Maybe you've arranged your schedule so that you'll be sobered up by the time you have to meet your clients. Maybe you've timed your high so that you will come down more or less when the plane does. You'll get no temperance speeches from me of *all* people. I have to point out two things, though.

The most disappointing property of alcohol or tranquilizers as antidotes to a really persistent fear of flying is that they don't always work. Unless you can knock yourself totally unconscious, your brain can still perceive the situation in which it finds itself. Depressants, for some people—particularly people who are ordinarily extremely controlled— cause the opposite reaction intended, knocking out whatever rational buffers a person has left and leaving a person at the mercy of a person's worst fears. Enough of this theoretical person! An example from life:

A forty-year-old investments counselor who took great pride in her ability to handle pressure without batting an eye finally had to fly for the first time after a lifetime of weaseling out of it by taking trains (unfortunately for her, she had to go to London, not on Amtrak's schedule). She figured a few martinis would get her through. After the third one she dissolved into uncontrollable weeping and spent the next two hours clutching the hands of a flight attendant, thus making herself the center of unwelcome attention and slowing down the dinner service. She didn't drink on the way back. She was still terrified, but her customary grace under pressure was allowed to wake up and assert itself.

Cautionary tale number two (and the last one you'll ever hear from me): A sales executive sitting next to me on a New York–Washington flight told me he'd just been promoted and hoped he would last longer in the job, which involved several flights a week, than the *last* guy. His former colleague, terrified of flying, had begun to drink before every flight so he could make himself get on, during every flight so he could bear it, and after every flight in the normal course of sales socializing. In eight months his performance deteriorated so badly he was fired.

Okay, that's it. Cheers.

9. It is now considered likely that the two hemispheres of your brain

are going about slightly different business all day long and into the night. Those of us who have trouble getting one personality in line may not wish to contemplate the possibility that we have *two*, but apparently each side has special areas of expertise. For our purposes here, the much-simplified breakdown is that your verbal, logical *left* brain is the one that knows the odds and understands the Bernoulli effect, and your nonverbal, emotional *right* brain is the one that strongly resents being shot into the air in a tin tube.

The structure of our brains hasn't really changed in many thousands of years, much less since Kitty Hawk. So you are effectively taking a hunter-gatherer organ, probably with an inherent evolutionary bias against heights, and putting it in a window seat where it can readily see that you're an awful long way from the old savannah.

For dull, unimaginative airline passengers in general, the left brain's logical assurances that a plane's as good as a truck are sufficient. The right brain says, in effect, "Duh—okay by me." But for some people made of brighter stuff, when the left brain says, "We're fine," the right brain says, "We're not fine, we're *in the frigging air.*" The right brain also seems to take, in general, a rather pessimistic view of things, as opposed to the bright, cheery good-do-bee left brain.

So, you want to do two things. You want to keep the left brain in control, and you want to keep the right brain pacified.

For example, reading, talking, writing, and counting are left-brain activities. Taking notes on what happens during the flight will keep your left brain active, and is useful for several other reasons. One, taking notes forces you to pay attention, and if you're forced to pay attention, you probably won't (an example of the well-known Study Hall Drowsiness Effect). If you get bored listening to the engines on this first flight, you're cured. Second, you can compare what happened on this flight with what happens on the next flight, no doubt finding a reassuring uniformity. Third, by trying to take notes about what is happening, you will be forcibly struck with how little is happening. Fourth, looking over your notes may give you an idea for a book.

Methodically ticking off the three hundred takeoff seconds is a left-brain activity.

Of course, the problem is usually that your left brain keeps getting distracted from its reading, talking, writing, and counting, by the right brain screaming for its mother. So an alternative approach is to occupy the right brain with something soothing. Drawing, singing, and walking around are all right-brain activities. Singing little songs to yourself is an exercise often prescribed by experts to entertain the right brain (if you sing little songs aloud, the flight attendant probably will not serve you another beer).

You might think of your right brain as a toddler to be pacified. When it gets bored with little songs, coloring books, and cookies, try walking it a little bit, just down the aisle and back. Please do not do this when the seat belt sign is on. If you turn your ankle, you won't get much sympathy from the flight attendant when you explain that you were just up walking your right brain.

Like a toddler, your right brain doesn't respond very well to verbal exhortations, like "Stop squirming." You have to convince it nonverbally. Concentrate on how firm the seat is, how much the upholstery feels like your cheapest armchair at home, how solid the floor is below your feet, how secure you are within the walls of the plane. Explaining why some people love to fly, psychiatrists have noted that the curved walls of a plane suggest the serene security of the womb. How they reconcile that with the phallic business is plainly out of my league. Don't dwell on this (unless, of course, you *want* to). The point is to persuade your right brain that you are doing nothing more dangerous than sitting in your cheapest armchair. Which happens to be true, never mind the view.

10. Some people who are afraid of flying have actually experienced an in-flight panic attack. They fear a repetition of that awful experience more than they fear crashing. Some researchers believe that many of the classic phobias, like agoraphobia and claustrophobia, are primarily the same fear with different triggers. Fear of the agonizing symptoms of a panic attack.

I am assuming that if you experience severe panic attacks, you will not rely on me to cure you of them. That would not be fair. People get a lot of money for curing panic attacks. However, many of us who are afraid of flying have mild versions of panic attacks, and you may want to keep the following in mind.

One, although panic attacks often include such *sensations* as difficult breathing and irregular heartbeat, no one dies of a panic attack. If you have one or two panic attacks, though, you certainly *feel* like you may die, and you'd just about rather do that than go through another panic attack, so you begin to avoid the merest brush with a similar situation.

If you're in a situation where you cannot avoid the circumstances you fear—strapped into a flying airplane, for example—suffering through the attack and discovering that you are still alive is supposed to be excellent therapy. So some experts recommend "impulse flying."

Impulse flying means that if you're passing an airport and feel suddenly strong enough, you should jump on the next plane to anywhere before you have time to reconsider. If you have a panic attack, you won't be able to avoid it and enduring it will probably prevent its occurrence next time.

Evidently, people with long-standing, severe phobias have been helped and in many cases completely cured once they realized they could get through panic attacks without lasting harm. But impulse flying still sounds like a pretty rough prescription to me. I would opt for the less harrowing approach of preparing yourself so that you avoid panic altogether.

A recent study involving people with acute agoraphobia (the word literally means "fear of the marketplace") indicates that hyperventilation—"overbreathing," the researchers call it—may be more than just another symptom of panic attacks.[1] Overbreathing may be the big daddy of symptoms, the one that *causes* all the other horrible sensations. When the researchers taught a group of agoraphobics how to breath through their diaphragms, the improvement was dramatic next time they were exposed to frightening situations. So if you feel as if you are beginning to panic, don't hyperventilate, for heaven's sake, you'll just drive all the carbon dioxide out of your lungs and give yourself all kinds of symptoms and blame your misery on flying when it was actually all your own fault.

Instead, breathe through your diaphragm (I was with a friend once, shortly before her wedding, when she began to hyperventilate. "Breathe through your diaphragm!" I urged. "I didn't bring it!" she choked. This is a true story). You don't need to know where your diaphragm is for this to work; simply breathe into your *stomach,* trying to keep your chest as still as possible. Keep your breathing slow and regular, and start counting again. Scientists who specialize in timing panic attacks say the worst symptoms rarely last for more than fifteen minutes. Granted, those fifteen minutes would feel more like five hundred, but the actual danger of twisting in the grip of a panic attack all the way to Honolulu is very small. Especially if you keep that carbon dioxide under control (and concentrate on Elvis Presley's ghost).

You should take this information about panic attacks in the spirit in which it is offered: only as a backup, like the oxygen masks which will in all likelihood never fall. If you have flown before without having a full-dress panic attack, chances are you're not going to have one now. If you have never flown, chances are you are not going to have one on your first flight, particularly if you have the information and preparation you now have. You know the Franklin Roosevelt quote that applies here.

11. I'll make a deal with you. If you write me a letter after your flight describing any sounds you heard that you didn't understand, or any sensations you felt that you considered unusual *(airplane*-related sensations; I don't want to hear about the crush you developed on the flight attendant), I'll write you back and explain them to you. If I can't figure out what they might have been, I'll find somebody who can. But you have to describe them *in detail.* Exactly what the sound was, at exactly which point in the flight, how long it lasted, where it seemed to originate, precisely what it reminded you of, whether or not you noticed any movement of the control surfaces on the wings as you were hearing it, the whole works. It's not so much that I'm desperate for pen pals. I'm just a living witness to how effectively a little careful, deliberate observation can take the sting out of an airplane flight. I think it may be more left-brain phenomena, but whatever it is, it may work for you, too.

Now, don't be *too* hard on me. Any single-spaced ten-page letter that starts, "Just wait till I get my hands on you" I'm going to toss, tear-stained, into the trash can.[2]

12. Since landing takes longer than takeoff, you may not want to use the same counting routine. From the first time the engines are slowed, you'd probably have to count to about 1,800. If you do plan to count all the way down, take the precaution of alerting somebody to wake you up when you're on the ground.

While it's true that over 50 percent of accidents in the last twenty-five years have happened in the final approach and landing phase, those numbers are somewhat weighted by accidents that occurred before the present sophisticated electronic precision-landing systems. But if you insist on knowing precisely when to worry, I guess this is as good a time as any.

While you're worrying, though, begin your relaxation exercise from the beginning, approximately thirty minutes before you're scheduled to land, which is probably close to the time you'll first notice a change in speed. I used to really *hate* this part. There always seemed to be so much surging forward followed by *hanging,* and thunderous rumbling followed by eerie silence. But you're in the home stretch, now. Stop, relax, focus. Listen carefully to the sounds so that you can (a) compare next time and (b) keep me busy calling pilots and asking, "Now, what do you think *this* might have been?" for the rest of my life.

Again, picture those planes you watched landing. And keep in mind that although it *sounds* like the engines are being turned off, the plane is not drifting in any sense of the word. You are still proceeding right smartly toward your destination, as anyone watching from the ground could plainly see. The plane really does not stop its controlled forward motion until it pulls up to the gate.

AFTER THE FLIGHT

1. Book another one. As soon as possible. Don't wait so long that you have to get yourself into shape all over again. Fly again so you can reinforce whatever gains you've made, and before you forget where your remaining in-flight trouble spots are. The next one will be easier to get through, and the one after that easier still, and pretty soon you won't just be getting through, you'll be *over.*

2. You know, I'd sort of like to hear from you if things went *better,* too. If I've made even a modest social contribution, I certainly want to know. It may happen, in the air on some stormy night, that I might have just the teeniest relapse, a momentary vision of kreplach dancing in my brain. I would like to be able to say, "Lord, these seven or eight people trusted me. Nobody's going to believe flying is safe if *I* don't make it."

Getting Over

The first flight I took after I began to write this book was the worst flying experience I ever had, bar none, even including the red-eye from Chicago where I had my brilliant, false clairvoyant vision of my footnote death, even including sputtering to Hilton Head on a wing and a Valium.

I had been on a plane, of course, when the idea for the book first came to me. I was a little tipsy but still miserable and I thought, I've got to do something about this, I can't live like this, maybe I should talk to somebody, or read a book or something. Maybe, the wine whispered, you should *write* a book. I felt better immediately. Research! That's the answer. Scientific inquiry. I'm a writer, I'll just write the thing myself. I will get to the bottom of this wretched phobia. I outlined the book on the spot, no more convinced than ever that I would live through the flight, but with an additional reason for hoping so.

Safely on the ground, I began rounding up the preliminary facts, talking to people, checking a few numbers. I found out there really wasn't another book like the book I wanted to write (or read) and I was pretty fired up. I began to have a wonderful time finding out about planes. I didn't actually have to *fly* in one until about two months later.

This, I was sure, was going to be a dead cinch. One in three million, I had it on the best authority. Engines never stopped. Wings could not fly wildly off on separate journeys. Waiting at the gate, I took the precaution of propitiating the terrible gods of airline flight by going through the usual motions, muttering the usual incantations: I could die today, these could be my last five minutes on earth, they could find my shoe, this very shoe I am looking at now, perched poignantly on smoking rubble. But I was muffling a secret smile. I've got this knocked. I know the *facts*.

I was fine all the way up to the takeoff run.

I didn't flee to the bathroom. I knew at last that I couldn't run there or anywhere, could not solve this. My fear could never be explained away. It didn't matter at all that now I *knew* how safe I was. Whatever I was afraid of didn't care. I realized that I really did not believe any more that the plane was going to crash. Apparently, all my research had accomplished nothing but the loss of that last reasonable illusion. I'd swindled myself out of a recognizable object for The Fear. I was scared to death and didn't even know any more of what. Just being there. Just falling. I was mortally afraid I was going to fall. Not the plane so much as just me.

I don't remember moving a muscle the entire two hours. I didn't know I was betraying how awful I felt, but after the plane landed the man next to me finally leaned over and said, "Are you all right?" I imagine I must have had an expression on my face similar to that of the dogs in their traveling cages borne forlornly around the luggage carousel. All hope is lost. Struggle is useless.

I decided to finish the book. I'd just have to leave me out of it. Not a very good testimonial, perhaps, that the author couldn't even cure *herself*, but nobody had to know, right? And surely nobody else was as deranged as I was. Most people would read the facts, which I would scrupulously collect and present, and that would be enough for most people. Normal people.

I had to do a great deal of flying as part of the research, not to mention getting to other places I had to go. I would begin each flight thinking, "I really cannot bear this." Sometime, I don't even known when, I started being able to get *through* a flight a little better. I had rather grandly adopted a spirit of scientific inquiry toward the whole operation, listening carefully for the minutest sounds, describing them precisely, noting the swings and pulses not only as possible harbingers of death but also as questions—must find out what causes that.

My notes were still decorated with sudden diagonal slashes where my pencil slid off the paper at a noise or a bump. Entire shakily scrawled paragraphs were devoted to how heavy or disjointed or unusual the plane felt, as if I thought the crash investigators might want to recover my notebook along with the black box. But every once in a while, somewhere in my research I'd find one fact or one technique that I would think about over and over during a flight, some number or explanation or story that seemed as real up there as when I read it or heard it.

One time in-flight I was staring at my green-white lunatic face in the bathroom mirror and the panic just sort of broke, like a raced engine might throw a rod. The overload switch just flipped over. *I can't be this scared any more right now.* I went out and took my seat and the plane landed and I went on about my business. Another time I was biting my cuticles down to blood, waiting for the plane to take off, getting myself ginned up, when I thought, I'm really too tired to be this crazy today, can't we just fly this one flight like a normal person?

Something about the whole enterprise was certainly changing, the drama was falling away, the experience getting a little less intense. I didn't want to think about it, though. I remembered the last time I got cocky.

A couple of years ago I was looking out the window of an airliner, toward sundown, wondering over the clouds getting red, the sky burning like a bonfire, even the wing grazed with pink, and I started thinking about the way fears seem to bear a little seed of their opposites, if desire is the opposite of fear. Vertigo is said to be at its black heart a desire to throw oneself down from a height, and agoraphobia a defense against what one truly wants to do out there in the marketplace. So what is fear of gathering speed, fear of leaving the ground? Maybe fear of staying in the air? Is it fear of falling, or fear of not falling? A desire for heights one feels unable to sustain? Didn't matter to me at that moment, although I've given it some thought since. Then, I just decided that the plane was meant to fly, and so was I, we were both aerodynamically correct. The plane wasn't meant to disappear unreasonably from the firmament, and neither was I.

It's been a long time since I felt anything more than a little passing nervousness on a plane. No apprehension I have now even remotely resembles that awful, persistent, nightmare panic. The difference is not only one of degree, but more like the difference between the bizarre darkness in a dream and the plain old darkness in your bedroom when you wake up. I am absolutely convinced that even if I were on a plane that experienced some major and very real difficulty, the terror I would feel would not be the same old one (it would be a real *big* one, though, I'm not *crazy*).

I had to find or figure out the facts and ideas and techniques in this book piecemeal, one by one, over a long and bumpy period of time. I hope it will be a little easier for you, finding them all in one place, but just as fear is partly irrational, I think the absence of fear is partly irrational, too. I certainly know a great deal more now about the bad things that have happened on planes than I ever did when I was afraid. I've read detailed accident reports, listened to countless scary stories, followed as carefully as I could the reasoned arguments of critics of the system. I can't altogether explain when or why I just began to feel more like the millions upon millions who will be safe than like the few who will ever be in danger. Nothing in the world outside had changed, just a small interior realignment, not entirely intellectual. I didn't even notice when it slipped into place.

I have friends who believe I'm only over my fear of flying as an accidental by-product of decisions I made in my life. Their theory is that during this period I coincidentally had to face up to the fact that a *lot* of things in my life were going to have to fly or crash. They figure once I'd taken *those* frightening risks, and hadn't altogether died, the planes I flew on could get off the ground a lot easier without the heavy freight of generic hesitation I'd carried on in the past. Maybe.

I agree that how long it takes to get *over* the fear of flying depends on how much what you are afraid of is flying. If it's really just planes, if it's even just crashes, I'm not too worried about you. You get over a fear when you decide, for whatever reason, to accept instead of resist the evidence, and the evidence about planes and crashes is pretty clear. And I agree that people who are suddenly afraid of flying are usually suddenly afraid of something in their lives, and people who have been afraid of flying for a long time usually have been afraid of something in their lives for a long time. But what's new? Who isn't? All the fears boil down to fear of living; what good does that do you as long as you're alive?

I also freely admit that you can finesse most risks on the ground. You can get out of practically anything, get married, get divorced, have children, leave your children behind, take another job, keep your old one, back down, back out. Get up in a plane, though, and everything's put back on your plate. Choke it down if you can. Simple cure for aerophobia, then—go forth, clear your conscience, set your life in order, avoid nothing, risk all, and presto, no white knuckles.

If that's the cure, I'd rather be afraid of flying my whole life. I never would have undertaken a cure like *that* on purpose. The truth is, I don't completely buy this whole theory that fixing your life fixes your fear. If anything, the "cures" worked in reverse, for me. I set out to take apart my fear of flying, just as a project, just to rid myself of one minor aggravation in life, just to make getting around a little easier. When I found out, to my great surprise, that I could actually do that, I thought maybe the same approach would work on some other things. Sometimes it did, sometimes it didn't. Flying in airliners is safe, you can easily afford to uncurl from the fetal position there. Risk/benefit ratios aren't usually quite that straightforward.

The first few flights I took without The Fear amazed me. I kept pinching myself. Now I have a hard time keeping any sense at all of how momentous flight is. I have to remind myself. Which I try always to do, because flight *is* momentous, splendidly so. I've become pretty casual about flying, but I don't think I'll ever take it for granted, and that, I think, is a great gift.

One I hope you will be able to give yourself.

Although at this point you may only be concerned about removing your fear, and becoming more like the other heedless travelers who think of flying with the same rush of emotion elicited by a trip on the crosstown bus, you might want to consider this: flying is not only nothing to be afraid of, it's also wonderful.

True, on the one hand you have holding patterns, delays, overbooking, baggage mix-ups, assembly line Danishes, and just about exactly enough room to cross your legs. But on the other hand, you have commuter marriages, commuter affairs, commuter one-night stands. All at once, if conditions are right! Hundreds of miles can vanish behind you in the time it takes to watch two or three bad sitcoms.

And true, our flying machines are burning an ocean of oil and spewing mighty clouds of jet smoke into the sky and having God-knows-what effect on the ozone layer. But you would have to have a very cold heart not to confess that flight has been one of mankind's longest obsessions, and there's something triumphant in the fact that we finally figured it out. Mastered it so completely, in fact, that almost anybody with the price of a ticket can go almost anywhere on earth through the air, miles above the ground, so effortlessly they don't even have to be awake.

If you have never flown, or have never flown without being so afraid you didn't want to look out the window because you were trying to pretend you were in your Subaru, you are missing something exquisitely beautiful. Few things so spectacular involve such small risk and so little effort. We're among the first generations in the long history of mankind to see the world from this angle (leaving *Chariots of the Gods* aside for the moment). If Keats could immortalize an urn, think what he could have done with the heart-stopping sights you can only see from the air. Assuming, with his imagination, we could have gotten him into the air.

It's possible that once you get yourself unclenched you may find you actually *want* to be in that lit, stupendous sky.

They say on the Concorde you can see the dark edge where the blue blurs into space, and you can see a curve to the earth. I want to see that someday. Our children will probably see even more splendid sights than that, and flying a mere 35,000 feet above the world will be as quaint as a sleigh ride. Only the most imaginative few will develop intractable fear of the Trans-Lunar Express.

John Gillespie Magee, the author of the poem "High Flight" that opened the last chapter, was a fighter pilot for the Royal Canadian Air Force during World War II, and he died at age nineteen, in his plane, over England. Commercial flight would probably have seemed pretty tame to him. You do not get quite the same sensation of flinging your eager craft through footless halls of air in a 747. The sanctity of space is routinely trespassed. They say of John Magee that he was reckless, wild, obsessed as much with the danger of flying as with the beauty. His superiors had often reprimanded him for taking unnecessary chances. A psychiatrist after the war interpreted Magee's line about touching the face of God as typical of the insolence and bravado of ace fliers.[1] Going our ordinary, buckled-up, commuter way across and back the radio-scanned, computer-monitored highways of the present-day sky is not very much like what John Magee did. There is none of the danger, and not much of the joy. But there is that long, delirious, burning blue. Flying is as scary as anything beautiful and powerful is. No more. No less. I wish you blue skies.

"The fear is gone now—not overcome nor reasoned away. It is gone because something else has taken its place; the confidence and the trust, the inherent belief in the security of land underfoot—now this faith is transferred to my plane, because the land has vanished and there is no other tangible thing to fix faith upon. Flight is but momentary escape from the eternal custody of earth."

Beryl Markham, *West with the Night*

APPENDICES

I. A SAMPLE HIERARCHY

Remember, this is just a sample. It helps to write out each step in your own personal hierarchy, because you want to take care to include how each step feels, sounds, smells (that first hot diesel blast smell of an airport was always good for provoking anxiety with me), what's scary about it, what you're afraid might be happening. You have to imagine these test flights *thoroughly,* attempting to recreate them in your imagination exactly as you experience them in life. Your hierarchy can, of course, have as many or as few steps in it as you want, but it really should start out with easy, not very scary stages, and work up to just about as scary as you can stand. But don't spend your entire desensitization on the preposterously unlikely; try to spend some time imagining your way through the routine aspects of the flight, too. You want to get ready to be relaxed through the things you *know* will happen, not just things you're afraid *might* happen.

1. Calling a travel agent/airline and making a flight reservation.
   Anxiety-provoking factor: 1½
2. Getting ready (packing, making preparations, and, probably, worrying) the night before the flight.
   Anxiety-provoking factor: 3
3. Driving to the airport.
   Anxiety-provoking factor: 3
4. Arriving at the airport.
   Anxiety-provoking factor: 4

5. Standing in ticket check-in line.
   Anxiety-provoking factor: 2½
6. Waiting in gate area.
   Anxiety-provoking factor: 4½
7. Boarding the flight.
   Anxiety-provoking factor: 5
8. Waiting in seat for takeoff.
   Anxiety-provoking factor: 5½
9. Plane begins to taxi toward takeoff point.
   Anxiety-provoking factor: 5½
10. Plane begins takeoff run.
    Anxiety-provoking factor: 7
11. Plane takes off and begins to climb.
    Anxiety-provoking factor: 8
12. Plane is cruising normally.
    Anxiety-provoking factor: 7½
13. Plane starts bumping in turbulence; seat belt sign goes on.
    Anxiety-provoking factor: 8
14. Something really bad happens (I told you, I'm not going to suggest *what*).
    Anxiety-provoking factor: 9 9/10
15. Something really bad doesn't happen, but eventually plane starts slowing down to land.
    Anxiety-provoking factor: 7½
16. Approach for landing is particularly bumpy; plane speeds up and slows down several times; there's bad weather in the area.
    Anxiety-provoking factor: 8½
17. Final stages of landing approach are over water; water seems very close outside window.
    Anxiety-provoking factor: 8
18. Plane touches down on runway.
    Anxiety-provoking factor: 2 (You're worried your luggage went to some other destination.)

II. A RELAXATION ROUTINE

(You may want to tape this, especially if you have a friend with a particularly soothing voice. Then you'd have a tape to take on the flight with you—if the soothing friend wasn't free to go along in person—and it would help focus you on relaxing. The important points are tensing each muscle group in turn, holding for a few seconds, and then relaxing.)

Start with your feet. Wiggle your toes and flex your feet, turning your toes in toward each other. Tense your feet and ankles as tightly as you can. Hold—slowly count, one thousand one, one thousand two, one thousand three, one thousand four—and relax. Let them go completely limp.

Now your calves up to your knees. First your left leg—tense, as hard as you can. Hold—one, two, three, four—and relax. Then your right leg. Tense, hold tight—one, two, three, four—relax.

Tighten your left thigh. Hold tight—one, two, three, four—then relax. Remember, count very slowly. Keep breathing, slowly and regularly. Now the right thigh. Clench, hard as you can, hold—one, two, three, four—and release. Let your legs go limp.

Take a deep breath. Breathe in—one, two, three, four—and breathe out, slowly, to the same rhythm.

Now tighten your stomach, as if somebody were going to hit you. Hold—one, two, three, four—and then let all the air go out in a rush and relax.

Clench your buttocks together, hard as you can, as if you could lift yourself up from the seat. Hold—count slowly—one, two, three, four—and release.

Take a deep breath. Your body from the waist down is completely limp, like a rag doll.

Now tense your rib cage; try to draw the two sides of your body together. Contract your whole upper body, curving your back. Hold—one, two, three, four—and then relax, fall back in your seat.

Push your shoulder blades together, tensing your upper back. Contract hard. Now hold—one, two, three, four—and relax, let your shoulders drop.

Take a deep breath. Breathe in—one, two, three, four—and let it out—one, two, three, four.

Now clench your right fist and tense your entire right arm, right up to the shoulder, so hard your elbow might shake. Hold it tensed—one thousand one, one thousand two, one thousand three, one thousand four—and relax. Again, let your shoulder drop.

Splay the fingers of your right hand. Hold your hand completely rigid, as tense as you can. Hold—one, two, three, four—and relax, shake your hand out like a dishrag, let it fall to your lap.

Clench your left fist, and clench your left arm hard, right up to the shoulder. Hold—one, two, three, four—and release.

Splay the fingers of your left hand. Hold it rigid—count one, two, three, four—and shake it out, let it fall limp.

Take a deep breath. Your entire body from the shoulders down is heavy and limp. Breathe in—one, two, three, four—and breathe slowly out—one, two, three, four.

Tense the muscles in your neck. This will draw up your shoulders a little bit. Hold tight—one, two, three, four—and release, let your shoulders drop.

Tense your face. Press your lips together hard and scrunch up your eyes. At home, make the most grotesque face possible. On the plane, make a less frightening contortion—lift your eyebrows as high as they'll go and make a huge yawn. Hold—one, two, three, four—and release. Relax your tongue. Relax your eyes. Feel the tension slowly dissolving out of your face.

Now focus on your legs, from your thighs to your toes. Any remaining tension flows down to your toes and out. One thousand one, one thousand two, one thousand three, one thousand four.

Start at your shoulders. Any remaining tension drains slowly down from your shoulders and out through your toes. One thousand one, one thousand two, one thousand three, one thousand four.

Focus on your right shoulder. Any remaining tension in your arm flows slowly down from your shoulder and out through your fingertips. Count slowly—one, two, three, four.

Focus on your left shoulder. Any remaining tension in your arm flows slowly down from your shoulder and out through your fingertips. One, two, three, four.

Now tip your head slowly, gently back. Take a deep breath. Any remaining tension in your face falls away. Bring your head back level. Rest it against the chair.

Take a deep breath—one, two, three, four. Let it out—one, two, three, four. Close your eyes, and imagine yourself floating in a turquoise pool, on a big comfortable raft, perfectly relaxed. The sun is warm on your face. Your fingertips trail in the water. You can hear the water gently splashing against the raft. If you open your eyes a crack you can see the sun glinting off the blue water. A soft little breeze plays over you. There isn't any tension anywhere in your body, you're stretched out, languid, floating, nothing to think about, all the time in the world, you're bathed in warm sun. Relaxed. Tranquil. Peaceful. Just floating.

YOU ARE NOW COMPLETELY IN MY POWER.

Just kidding. You are now probably half asleep. But now, completely relaxed and floating and safe, is the time to think about whichever stage of the flight you've planned for today. Imagine it carefully. Notice how —and where—the thoughts tense you up again. After a few minutes in your imaginary plane, relax, come back to floating in your azure pool. And then get up and rejoin your life already in progress.

III. A SUMMARY OF FATAL U.S. AIRLINE ACCIDENTS, 1974–85*

Fatal accidents occurring in the United States involving major domestic carriers on regularly scheduled jet passenger flights. The worst aviation accident in history, at Tenerife, Canary Islands, is included although it did not take place in the United States. Not included are the four incidents on U.S. airlines during this period that resulted in single fatalities: an unattended infant in 1974; a flight attendant killed in a galley accident in 1981; a passenger who fell from an airstair in 1981, and a snow-sweeper operator in 1983.

* This chart is based on my own analysis of NTSB accident reports.

Carrier/Flight No.	Model	Place/Date	Fatalities	Survivors

1974

1. Eastern 212   DC-9-31   Charlotte, N.C.   71   11
                                September 11,
                                1974

Controlled collision with ground in patchy fog about three miles short of the runway at Douglas Municipal Airport; lack of altitude awareness during non-precision landing approach due to problems with cockpit discipline and failure to follow prescribed procedures; terrain and altitude warnings were not heeded.

2. TWA 514   727-231   Berryville, Va.   92   0
                            December 1,
                            1974

Controlled collision with hill about twenty-five miles outside Dulles International Airport in low clouds and gusty winds; communication problems with air traffic control, confusion about terminology; failure to follow prescribed procedures; inadequate charts.

1975

3. Eastern 66   727-225   Jamaica, N.Y.   112   12
                              June 24, 1975

Very strong thunderstorm/microburst encountered during landing at JFK International Airport; plane crashed into runway approach lights; continued use of runway when air traffic control and crew should have been aware of severe weather hazard; at least four previous flights had experienced severe wind shears across runway; improper decision to continue landing.

1976

1977

4. Pan Am 1736   747   Tenerife,   326 (248   70
                          Canary Islands   on other
                          March 27, 1977   plane)

Struck on runway by Dutch KLM 747 taking off in limited visibility weather conditions; apparent misunderstanding by KLM pilot of departure controller's instructions. Accident investigated by Spanish authorities.

Carrier/Flight No.	Model	Place/Date	Fatalities	Survivors
5. Southern Airways 242	DC-9-31	New Hope, Ga. April 4, 1977	62 (8 on ground)	23

Attempted emergency landing on highway through town of New Hope; had been scheduled to land at Hartsfield–Atlanta International Airport; extreme thunderstorm, massive ingestion of hail and water which, in coordination with throttle movements, induced severe stall and major engine damage; failure of company dispatch to provide up-to-date weather information; crew's reliance on radar to penetrate extremely hazardous thunderstorm; limitations of air traffic control to provide for dissemination of timely weather report.

1978

6. Continental 603	DC-10-10	Los Angeles, Calif. March 1, 1978	2	198

Overran runway at Los Angeles International Airport following rejected take-off; sequential failure of two tires, resulting in failure of a third at critical point in takeoff; collapse of left landing gear and subsequent fire over left wing area; wet runway and additional loss of braking after tire failure.

7. National 193	727-235	Pensacola, Fla. May 8, 1978	3	55

Plane came to rest in about twelve feet of water in Escambia Bay about three miles from runway at Pensacola Regional Airport; improper landing procedures by pilot and copilot; required altitude and approach performance callouts not performed; improper procedures by air traffic controller; GPWS sounded but was mistakenly turned off due to miscommunication in cockpit.

8. Pacific Southwest Airlines 182	727-214	San Diego, Calif. September 15, 1978	135 (9 on ground)	0

Collision with small plane about three miles outside Lindbergh Field while approaching to land; Cessna apparently had varied from course last instructed by air traffic control; PSA crew had been advised of small plane's location, and reported at one point that the small plane was in sight, but they apparently thought it had passed clear of them; official report cited "failure of flight crew to comply with provisions of maintain-visual-separation clearance, including requirement to inform controller when they no longer had other aircraft in sight"; ALPA later presented data to indicate PSA crew had actually sighted a *different* Cessna and had never been aware of the plane with which they collided shortly after; also officially cited as a contributing factor were air traffic control procedures in effect at the time that authorized controllers to use visual separation although radar separation capabilities were available; the possibility of crew fatigue after an unusually heavy flight schedule has been noted, but was not cited in the official NTSB report.

Carrier/Flight No.	Model	Place/Date	Fatalities	Survivors
9. United 173	DC-8-61	Portland, Ore. December 28, 1978	10	179

Crashed into wooded area about six miles from the runway during approach to Portland International Airport after holding at low altitude for about one hour; approach was delayed while crew dealt with a faulty landing gear and prepared for emergency landing; failure to monitor fuel consumption and to respond properly to low fuel level led to fuel exhaustion; investigation indicated plane probably could have landed safely about thirty minutes after gear malfunction.

1979

10. American 191	DC-10-10	Chicago, Ill. May 25, 1979	271	0

Crashed into open field about 4,600 feet beyond end of runway at Chicago's O'Hare International Airport; maintenance-induced damage led to separation of engine and pylon at critical point during takeoff from O'Hare airport, and resulted in damage to warning systems and wing control surfaces, causing asymmetrical stall and roll.

1980

1981

1982

11. Air Florida 90	737-222	Washington, D.C. January 13, 1982	74 (4 on ground)	5

Crashed into 14th Street Bridge shortly after takeoff from National Airport during blizzard; several improper deicing ground procedures during lengthy delay before takeoff; several improper deicing procedures by flight crew; resulting faulty engine readings led to insufficient thrust for takeoff conditions; takeoff was continued although crew several times noted anomalous readings; crew apparently unaware that 737 particularly sensitive to contamination of wing control surfaces by ice or snow; pitch-up combined with lack of sufficient thrust led to stall; crew inexperienced particularly in winter conditions; no runway distance markers; improper procedure by air traffic control.

Carrier/Flight No.	Model	Place/Date	Fatalities	Survivors
12. World Airways 30H	DC-10-30CF	Boston, Mass. January 23, 1982	2	210

Ran off icy runway, into shallow water of Boston Harbor, after landing; two passengers apparently drowned (their bodies were never found); failure of airport management to assess runway conditions; failure of air traffic control to transmit most recent reports from other pilots; crew's decision to maintain excessive speed for conditions.

| 13. Pan Am 759 | 727-235 | Kenner, La. July 9, 1982 | 145 (8 on ground) | 0 |

Encountered microburst during takeoff from New Orleans International Airport; struck a line of trees about two thousand feet beyond runway, at altitude of about fifty feet; crew was aware that low-level wind shear alerts had been occurring around the airport, but NTSB cited limitations of current ground-based wind-shear detection technology.

1983

1984

1985

| 14. Delta 191 | L-1011 | Dallas, Texas August 2, 1985 | 137 (1 on ground) | 27 |

Encountered most severe microburst documented in aircraft accident investigations, during landing at DFW International Airport, and crashed about six thousand feet short of runway; decision made to continue landing was faulted; weather information from other pilots, weather centers, and air traffic control not forwarded to crew.

From 1974 through 1985, U.S. carriers enplaned over 3,387,000,000 passengers in scheduled service on about 61 million flights.

IV. WHERE TO WRITE

In addition to the organizations listed below, there are two other places where a well-aimed letter from a concerned airline passenger would be a very useful contribution to aviation safety: your own senator or congressperson, and the airline you fly most frequently. Your representatives in Washington regularly hear about safety issues from the organizations listed below and many others, and (luckily) their "special" interests usually coincide with ours, but it doesn't hurt to remind our elected officials that they have a few plain old airline passengers in their constituency, too. As for airlines, you have a lot to choose from; let them know you consider safety when you're choosing. They'll probably be glad to hear it. Most airlines have extensive safety programs and remarkable records which they would be (certainly *should* be) delighted to tell you about.

And next time you get worried about air traffic controllers or FAA inspectors, fire off a letter to Secretary of Transportation Elizabeth Dole, 400 Seventh Street, S.W., Washington, D.C. 20590. She's their boss.

Committee on Commerce, Science, and Transportation
Subcommittee on Aviation
United States Senate
The Honorable Wendell Ford, Chairman
428 Hart Senate Building
Washington, D.C. 20510

Committee on Public Works and Transportation
Subcommittee on Aviation
United States House of Representatives
The Honorable Norman Mineta, Chairman
2251 Rayburn House Building
Washington, D.C. 20515

Air Line Pilots Association
Aviation Research and Education Foundation
535 Herndon Parkway
P.O. Box 569
Herndon, Va. 22070

Aviation Consumer Action Project
P.O. Box 19029
Washington, D.C. 20036
(For $2, ACAP will send you its booklet "Facts and Advice for
Airline Passengers.")

Flight Safety Foundation
5510 Columbia Pike
Arlington, Va. 22204-3194

Air Transport Association
1709 New York Avenue, N.W.
Washington, D.C. 20006

Aircraft Owners and Pilots Association
421 Aviation Way
Frederick, Md. 21701

International Airline Passengers Association
4301 Westside Drive
P.O. Box 660074
Dallas, Tx. 75266-0074

And, once again, the FAA's air safety consumer hot line is 800-FAA-
SURE.

Programs for Fearful Fliers

It will not hurt my feelings (much) if you decide you need a formal class to deal with your fear of flying. For some people, the group support and the in-depth approach are absolutely invaluable. All of these programs come highly recommended, and have had impressive success rates. If you have a deep-seated, long-standing clinical phobia, of course, you may be best off with a professional advising you about which formal treatment would suit you.

U.S. Air Fearful Flyers Program
Box 100
Glenshaw, Pa. 15116
412-486-5917
(Or call U.S. Air's local sales office.)

Seven-week course (one night a week) and one-hour graduation flight; held in various cities; $195 course fee includes a personal relaxation tape and other materials.

SOAR (Seminars on Aeroanxiety Relief)
P.O. Box 747
Westport, Ct. 06881
800-332-7359

Complete course consists of Phase 1, instruction on cassette tapes ($285, or $95 per section) for use at home, and an optional Phase 2, an airport workshop and graduation flight ($165), held in various cities.

Freedom from Fear of Flying
2021 Country Club Prado
Coral Gables, Fl. 33134
305-261-7042

Founded by Captain T. W. Cummings, widely considered the "dean" of fearful fliers' instruction, the course usually consists of four three-hour evening meetings ($285, including the preparatory tapes and material), and an optional graduation flight (cost varies); held in various cities.

Phobia Society of America
133 Rollins Avenue
Suite 4B
Rockville, Md. 20852-4004
301-231-9350

If you send PSA a stamped self-addressed legal-sized envelope, they'll forward information about phobia treatment resources in your area.

Roundhouse Square Phobia Treatment Center
1444 Duke Street
Alexandria, Va. 22314
703-836-7130

The costs will vary for this intensive sixteen-week course, including both individual and group counseling (probably in the $2,000 range); Roundhouse Square, of course, deals with many other phobias in addition to flight phobias.

Fear of Flying Clinic, Inc.
1777 Borel Place
Suite 300
San Mateo, Ca. 94402
415-341-1595

Two types of courses are held: a nine-week clinic, or a two-weekend clinic; fee for either is $395. Fear of Flying Clinic has branches in Seattle and Australia, and can provide referrals for courses in other parts of the United States, as well as abroad.

Phobia Center of Dallas–Ft. Worth
4307 Newton
Suite 11
Dallas, Tx. 75219
214-522-6181

In addition to its programs dealing with other phobias, the Phobia Center offers a special program for fearful fliers, usually consisting of two weekends (four eight-hour days' total) and a graduation flight; cost varies, but is generally in the $500 range.

Acknowledgments

The following people deserve most of the credit for anything I've gotten right—but none of them had any control whatsoever over the final product, so if you find a mistake, you can be sure it's entirely mine.

My debt to John O'Brien, Director of the Engineering and Air Safety Department of the Air Line Pilots Association, is particularly large. ALPA is like King Solomon's mines as far as information about airline flight is concerned, and any nuggets I've been able to bear away I owe mostly to Mr. O'Brien's unfailingly generous assistance. I'd also like to thank especially Bill Hammond, Bob Hall, Pablo Santamaria, and Dreama Yeager at ALPA, and the participants in ALPA's 1986 Air Safety Forum in Washington, D.C.—I didn't manage to talk to *quite* all 350 of them, but the three days I spent there were an invaluable education.

Ed Wood, Director of Engineering and Maintenance at the Flight Safety Foundation, went above and beyond the call of duty to check facts for me, provide background material I've referred to so often that it's dog-eared, and in general answer my questions plus the ones I *should* have asked.

Fred Farrar at the Federal Aviation Administration's Washington, D.C., headquarters was a gracious guide through a maze where I could easily have been lost and never heard from again. Special thanks also to Peter Schenk of FAA's Data Branch, and to Mary Ransom and Bill Bays of the FAA Main Library. Jim Dwyer of the Regional Air Traffic Control Center in Leesburg, Virginia, should probably write a book himself, but I'd really rather have him directing traffic, and I'm grateful he was there to vector me through a dismayingly complex subject.

It's too bad for fearful fliers (but lucky for me) that they all can't take part in U.S. Air's excellent Fearful Flyers Program, conducted with great skill and caring by Carol Stauffer, M.S.W., and Captain Frank Petee. I appreciate the assistance of Nancy Vaughan of U.S. Air. And to Patti Luongo and the passengers and crew of Flight 7001 of the Pittsburgh Flyers Club, thanks for letting me share a remarkable evening. It was a privilege to fly with you.

I am indebted to Captain Tom Bunn, founder and president of Seminars on Aeroanxiety Relief (SOAR), who gave me the key to a treasurehouse of information and insight about the fear of flying; I'm sure the hundreds who have taken his extraordinary course feel the same way.

And the following people very generously spent time helping me understand a little about what they know a *lot* about: William Luckie of Lockheed International; Tom Cole and Jack Campbell at the Boeing Company; Elaine Bendell at Douglas Aircraft Company; Chris Witkowski of the Aviation Consumer Action Project; Dr. Robert DuPont, founding president of the Phobia Society of America and director of the Washington Center for Behavioral Medicine; Jerilyn Ross of the Roundhouse Square Phobia Treatment Center; Gil Clark of the National Hurricane Center and Tommy Thomas of the National Oceanic and Atmospheric Administration's Aircraft Operations; Neal Savoy, FAA/Long Beach; Gary Killian and Ivan Connelly, FAA/Seattle; Diane Kirk, FAA/Boston; Dr. Angelo Mielle, Rice University; Susan Caperton of the International Airline Passengers Association; Guy Gaddis of the University of Michigan's Transportation Research Institute; and Frank Smith of Transportation Policy Associates. To Pam Stephens of Northwest Orient and Bill Campbell of Pacific Southwest Airlines, a special thank you for staying "on call."

I am grateful to Dr. Lawrence A. Brain of the Psychiatric Institute of Washington for reading a draft version; his wise advice has made many improvements possible. Thomas Boswell also read an early draft, and his comments were like a master class in how to write *anything*, but that is only one of his many veteran-to-rookie kindnesses to me. And before there was a book at all, the title *White Knuckles* originated in the fertile brain of Patty Barlett.

For their energy and expert counsel—but most of all for understanding me so well and being so much fun to work with—I thank my agents, Ann Sleeper and Raphael Sagalyn. I owe a great deal to Kathy Rowe, who launched this book at Doubleday, and to Les Pockell, who guided it safely through, working wonders for the book and its author. In fact, considering the wonderful support, encouragement, and good sense I've enjoyed from everyone connected with this book, it should be a masterpiece. Unfortunately, they couldn't write it for me, which is the only excuse I have.

This list may seem long to you, but I'm afraid the list of those I am leaving out is even longer—not just the many aviation and psychology experts who have helped me understand my subject, but, indispensably, the friends and siblings who regularly save my life, and all the innocent strangers I've waylaid on planes, whose stories I have shamelessly stolen.

The only thing for which I can take sole and undisputed credit is my inspired choice of Willard and Margaret Schmidt as parents. The rest has been easy.

Notes

PREFACE

1. The numbers cited for total worldwide airline fatalities and accidents in 1985—2,109 and thirty-one, respectively—are based on statistics compiled by *Flight International* magazine, reported in the January 25, 1986, issue. These numbers include scheduled and nonscheduled air transport passenger flights and regional/commuter passenger flights. The International Civil Aviation Organization (ICAO), using slightly different criteria, reports a preliminary 1985 count of 1,067 fatalities in twenty-two accidents in scheduled air services for ICAO Contracting States, excluding the U.S.S.R. It's interesting to note that, according to ICAO reports, turbojet aircraft operations—about 95 percent of total scheduled traffic—accounted in 1985 for seven accidents worldwide, while turbo-propeller and piston-engine aircraft—about 5 percent of total volume—accounted for fifteen accidents. At least one of the reasons for this difference is the superior reliability of the turbojet engine.

CHAPTER ONE

1. The observation that flying is about twenty-nine times safer than driving is based on statistics reported in the June 1985 Department of Transportation document "National Transportation Statistics" (DOT-TSC-RSPA-85-5): per million passenger miles, the motor vehicles fatality rate was 0.00857, or approximately 28.6 times higher than the air carrier (including air taxis and commuters) fatality rate of 0.0003. The bus transportation fatality rate was 0.00130 per million passenger miles; the Class I railroad fatality rate was 0.09635, making flying quite a bit safer than *those* transportation modes, too.

Another way of comparing the safety of different kinds of transportation was used by the National Safety Council and reported in *Accident Facts, 1985 Edition*. Based on 1983 figures, this study concluded that the passenger death rate per *one hundred* million passenger miles was .98 for cars and taxis; .04 for buses; .04 for passenger trains; and .01 for scheduled airlines. (Incidentally, as you can tell, this study and the NTSB statistics cited above are using different measures.)

You should keep in mind that these figures are for general comparison only —the numbers change from year to year and the criteria used depend on the design of the report. But in the years when major airlines suffer zero fatalities, motor vehicles still account for roughly fifty thousand deaths a year, so even we nonstatisticians can draw our own reasonable conclusions.

2. Congressman Mineta's quote is from his address to the Flight Safety Foundation's Cabin Safety Conference and Workshop, December 11–14, 1984.

3. 1985 highway transportation fatalities are based on preliminary National Transportation Safety Board (NTSB) estimates. The general breakdown of major categories was: highway fatalities, 44,500 (including pedestrians, 7,756); grade crossing, 574; railroad, 535; recreational marine fatalities, 1,100; aviation (including commuters, air taxis, and charters, as well as scheduled airlines), 644; general aviation, 937.

4. Figures for fatalities and disabling injuries in the home and workplace are from *Accident Facts, 1985 Edition,* published by the National Safety Council.

For several decades there have been an average of around 20,000 homicides a year in the United States, about a third occurring among family members. A 1985 study by the U.S. Bureau of Justice Statistics indicates that in general an American has an approximately 1-in-133 chance of being murdered, in an entire lifetime; 1-in-10,000 in a given year; a 1-in-31 lifetime chance of being involved in a violent crime other than murder. The lifetime chances of being murdered are, for white men, 1-in-131; for white women, 1-in-369; for black men, 1-in-21; for black women, 1-in-104. The risk estimates are based on 1982 figures.

The 1-in-260,000 chance of seeing a starter pitch a complete perfect baseball game is cited in the book *The Odds on Virtually Everything,* compiled by the editors of Heron House, published by Putnam, 1980.

5. The estimates throughout the book of daily departures, daily passenger counts, annual total scheduled departures, and annual totals of passengers enplaned on scheduled air carrier flights are based on numbers compiled by the Air Transport Association, and reported in their annual reports of the U.S. scheduled airline industry. The most recent report, issued in June 1986 and reflecting 1985 figures, shows approximately 380 million passengers enplaned on about 5,685,000 scheduled flights.

6. The estimates of fatalities and fatal accidents from 1974 through 1985 involving large turbojets flown by major domestic carriers on regularly scheduled passenger flights in the continental United States are based on my own analysis of NTSB accident statistics and briefs for the period.

7. The estimate of 40 million fearful fliers is really pretty conservative; the difficulty in citing a precise number lies in the fact that the researchers in most

major studies make a distinction between "fear" and "anxiety," with rather more agreement on how many are "afraid" than on how many are "anxious." Perhaps the most recent systematic national investigation of the prevalence of fear of flying among adult Americans was sponsored by the Boeing Company ("Fear of Flying: Impact on the U.S. Air Travel Industry," Robert D. Dean and Kerry M. Whitaker, 1980). The study merged the data from several surveys and estimated that 25.1 million adult Americans are "afraid" of flying; but it also estimated perhaps 12.6 percent (about 19 million) of the general adult population have some "anxiety" about flying. The data admits of several interpretations about how severe this anxiety is, how many of these people continue to fly, and so forth.

One survey cited indicates that 13.8 percent of people who have flown on a commercial aircraft are "anxious" in some degree about flying. Since roughly 70 percent of adult Americans have flown at some time, I've used the figure of about 15 million "anxious" fliers—but that's my own interpretation of the numbers, and I don't mean to suggest that the study above broke it down that way.

CHAPTER TWO

1. Richard L. Taylor, the pilot and writer who is quoted on the subject of airliners' stability, is the author of many books about flying, but if you're interested in a clearly written, basic guide to the principles of flight, his book *Understanding Flying*, Delacorte Press, 1977, is a great one. Though aimed primarily at private pilots of light planes, it certainly helped *me* understand flying.

2. You can get more information on the Pinch Hitters Program basic flight course by contacting the Aircraft Owners and Pilots Association (AOPA), 421 Aviation Way, Frederick, Md. 21701, 800-638-3101. The course usually costs $195, and is conducted in cities all over the country; if you can get at least six people together who want to take the class, AOPA says they'll find an instructor for you in your area. They also say they've taken more than one fearful flier and turned him or her into a flying enthusiast by way of this program.

CHAPTER THREE

1. Sources for the information about Ground Proximity Warning System accidents include an article in the March 1986 issue of *Callback*, the monthly bulletin of NASA's Aviation Safety Reporting System (ASRS), which summarized several ASRS investigations into the problems of controlled flight toward terrain, and the performance of terrain warning systems; a discussion of the then-new GPWS system in the April 11, 1977, issue of *Time* magazine; and my own analysis of NTSB accident briefs.

2. The special NTSB safety study on alcohol use among pilots involved in

fatal accidents, quoted in this chapter, is "Statistical Review of Alcohol-Involved Aviation Accidents," May 1, 1984.

3. The figures for average flight hours of major airline pilots hired in 1985 are estimated by the Future Aviation Professionals of America, based on their most recent annual surveys of pilot experience. They also estimate that new hires take, on average, a minimum of eight years to become captains. In the official report of the investigation into the 1982 Air Florida accident, the NTSB stated that its "informal survey" of major airlines indicated that pilots upgrading to captain had served an average of fourteen years as first or second officers with the same carrier (in contrast with the Air Florida Flight 90 captain, who became a 737 captain after only about two years' turbojet experience; Air Florida, as you probably know, is no longer in business).

A more complete discussion of airline safety statistics in the context of deregulation can be found in the FAA's "Annual Report on the Effect of Airline Deregulation on the Level of Air Safety," the most recent issued in January 1986.

The safety figures cited in this chapter regarding regional airlines were compiled by the Regional Airline Association.

4. About microbursts: The relative "powerfulness" of a microburst is, like everything else about them, a complicated scientific question. The comparison I've used is based on "maximum wind velocity differential": for the 1983 Andrews Air Force Base microburst, 294 feet per second; for the 1985 Dallas microburst involving Delta Flight 191, 125 feet per second. The Dallas microburst, however, is still being analyzed, and apparently had some highly unusual characteristics.

To say I am a nonscientist is like saying I am a non-Olympic medalist, and I sincerely appreciate the heroic efforts of Dr. Angelo Mielle of Rice University and Captain Bill Melvin of Delta Airlines, both distinguished experts in the field, to explain a few of the intricacies of microburst phenomena to me. Other sources for this section include presentations made at ALPA's 1986 Air Safety Forum by Dr. Mielle and Dr. Fernando Caracena of the National Oceanic and Atmospheric Association; "Lessons Learned from Wind Shear Encounters," a presentation to the Flight Safety Foundation, June 14, 1985, by Charles R. Higgins of the Boeing Company; Captain Melvin's March 1986 article in *Airline Pilot* magazine, "Flying Through Microbursts"; and articles in *Science News,* September 3, 1983 ("Windshear: Progress but no solution"), and *Natural History,* March 1986 ("An Ill Wind").

5. The references in this chapter and others to the percentage of accidents due to various causes since 1960, and to the percentage of accidents occurring during various phases of flight, are based in part on the Flight Safety Foundation report "Two Decades of Air Carrier Jet Operation," by Edward C. Wood and George P. Bates, an analysis of the accident record of the world fleet of air carrier jet aircraft from 1960–81.

6. The criteria that aircraft have to meet for certification are extremely exhaustive and complex; although to the best of my knowledge the generalizations I've used are accurate, I certainly don't want to leave you the impression that there's one simple test, such as withstanding 2 g's, for overall structural soundness. Some of an aircraft's parts and structures must be able to withstand much more than that, and it's not just a question of "how much," it's also a question of "under what conditions"—precise limits are set for various speeds, weights, and situations—and "from what direction"—for example, under emergency landing conditions a structure might have to withstand a general load factor of 2 g's, 9 g's for forward loading, 1½ g's for sideways loading, and 4½ g's for downwards loading. There are also rigorous "gust loads" tests that airliners must satisfy, demonstrating that they can fly safely at various speeds through gusts and downdrafts more severe than they are likely to encounter in an entire service lifetime (remember that even in microburst-related accidents, the serious damage to the plane wasn't from the downdraft; it was caused by the impact with the ground when the plane was too low to recover). In general, the stress a structure might encounter during "ultimate" (read: "not very likely") conditions is calculated, and then the rules factor in one-and-a-half *times* that as a safety margin, and then the manufacturers make sure it's at *least* that good.

7. The study of turbulence-related injuries over the period of 1977–84 was among those discussed in the report "Occupant Injuries Aboard Air Carrier Aircraft as a Result of Turbulence," presented by Nora C. Marshall, Transportation Safety Specialist, NTSB, to the Flight Safety Foundation's Cabin Safety Conference, December 1984.

8. Now, you understand that when I tell you stories about my poor 1972 Camaro, I'm not saying anything bad about Camaros in *general*, right? Considering the treatment my car got, it's a miracle of engineering that it ever ran at all, believe me.

9. Most of the information specifically about performance of the JT8D series engine is from testimony given by William G. Robertson, Executive Vice President of the Commercial Products Division, Pratt & Whitney, before the Aviation Subcommittee of the Senate Committee on Commerce, Science, and Transportation, April 15, 1986.

10. My description of the July 23, 1983, Gimli, Canada, incident is based on several sources, including stories from pilots (not the ones involved), but the facts are checked against a number of press reports, especially those in the always thorough and authoritative *Aviation Week and Space Technology* magazine. I made up the "quote" about the tractor pull, but you probably guessed that, didn't you?

11. The figure about the dramatic reduction in holding patterns was stated by Jack Ryan, Director of Air Traffic Operations, FAA, before the Senate Aviation Subcommittee on October 1, 1985.

12. The engine fell off an American Airlines 727 on April 16, 1985. Appar-

ently a leaky lavatory had, over the course of many flights, gradually caused an ice buildup. I heard a well-known comedian refer to this ice buildup as a "p__berg."

13. According to the official accident report NTSB-AAR-75-2, a man from Beaumont, Texas, was lost from a National Airlines DC-10 near Albuquerque, New Mexico, on November 3, 1973. Despite a massive search, his body was never found. At 39,000 feet, the plane's number three engine fan assembly disintegrated, and fragments penetrated the other engines, the right wing, and the body of the plane, and the damage caused a severe cabin decompression. One cabin window was struck by a fragment, and the entire window assembly was separated from the plane. The investigators determined that the seat belt of the passenger sitting next to the window had been fastened, but, according to their measurements, only very loosely. The plane landed safely nineteen minutes later; twenty-five of the passengers aboard were treated for minor injuries —smoke inhalation, ear problems, minor cuts.

The magnitude of the engine failure, the massive damage that followed, the precisely localized and catastrophic loss of one complete window assembly— these were each wildly unlikely; however, the sequence of events in the disintegrated engine itself (a General Electric CF6-60) was even more baffling. That sequence was analyzed in the most minute detail, but the investigators kept coming down to the fact that the engine had suddenly accelerated to an abnormally high fan speed, which had in turn set up a destructive vibration, and no one was able to explain what could make a jet engine do that. According to the report, "At 39,000 feet, under a normal cruising environment, it is difficult to conceive of any condition under which engine limits could be exceeded, even with maximum throttle lever travel." No engine had done it before, even under testing conditions much more extreme. Immediately before the malfunction, the crew apparently had been doing what I can only describe as fooling with the engines, but, as damning as that sounds, their actions could not account for the problem. The Board took the opportunity, in the report, to caution against deviations from established procedure (although it's hard to believe any professional pilot needed much reminding on this point).

When something happens to a plane that is virtually impossible and that has never happened before, the authorities do not, thank God, chalk it up to freak chance and continue as before. That this bizarre incident happened once was bad enough; if it had happened twice there would be a lot more than 40 million fearful fliers among the airlines' potential customers. By the time the official report came out, a number of additional safeguards had already been introduced to engines and engine testing, to increase further an engine's ability to withstand even once-in-a-lifetime situations without endangering the plane or anybody on it. Just as one example, a device for containing engine blades if they do malfunction was redesigned to provide each blade with a retaining capability of sixty thousand pounds, compared to the eighteen-thousand-pound capability of the engine involved in the accident.

You might think turbojet engines were so reliable and sophisticated now that there wasn't much left to do to improve them, but the major manufacturers—Pratt & Whitney, GE, Rolls-Royce—continue to develop new series and new technology. GE, for instance, has been a pioneer in the research for strengthening engine shrouds with the space-age material used in bulletproof vests.

14. The U.S. hijacking figures were taken from the FAA's "Semiannual Report to Congress on the Effectiveness of the Civil Aviation Security Program, January 1–June 30, 1985," issued in November 1985.

CHAPTER FOUR

1. I have many people to thank for explanations and examples of the airline certification, testing, and maintenance process, not only from the manufacturers but from the FAA and other organizations, especially ALPA and the Flight Safety Foundation; some of the facts and figures are from the extensive testimony given on the subject before the Senate Subcommittee on Aviation, April 15, 1986, by Jim Burnett, Chairman of the NTSB; Anthony Broderick, FAA Associate Administrator for Aviation Standards; Benjamin A. Cosgrove, Vice President of Engineering, the Boeing Company; Dale Warren, Director of Design and Technology, McDonnell Douglas Corporation; and Robert W. Baker, Senior Vice President of Operations, American Airlines. And anyone interested in a fairly technical but fascinating view of what's involved in flight testing a new aircraft should look up Benjamin M. Elson's article about the 757 and 767, "Boeing Flight Testing Two New Aircraft at Same Time to Meet Certification Goal," *Aviation Week and Space Technology,* February 15, 1982.

2. Although several pilots had told me versions of the story of one man and his lawn chair, I don't think I really believed it until a reporter from the Long Beach *Press-Telegram* was kind enough to look up some of the old stories and read me the highlights over the phone. But I particularly appreciate the assistance of Neal Savoy of the Long Beach FAA, who originally investigated the incident.

CHAPTER FIVE

1. The safety record of major airlines flying large jets in scheduled passenger service is usually the best in aviation, for many reasons—the rules governing their operations are especially strict, their standards for personnel qualifications, experience, and training are high, their maintenance programs are well funded, their equipment is among the best, and so forth—but they actually represent a very small percentage of total flight operations. In addition to regional airlines, commuter airlines, air taxis, charters, and cargo operations,

about 98 percent of the planes flying in the United States fall under the category of general aviation, flown by private pilots and businesses. And, particularly compared with the huge volume of flight hours involved, each of these categories also has an impressive safety record.

The following are figures for 1985, according to the National Transportation Safety Board (as a point of comparison, the ten-year average rate of fatal accidents per 100,000 departures for scheduled air carriers is 0.055):

For nonscheduled, or charter, flying, the 3 fatal accidents in 1985 produced a rate of 1.887 fatal accidents per 100,000 departures. There had been no nonscheduled carrier fatal accidents in 1984, nor in five of the past ten years. The Gander, Newfoundland, crash involving a charter carrying American soldiers accounted for 256 of the 329 fatalities in 1985 nonscheduled operations.

For commuter operations, the 1985 fatal accident rate was 0.25 per 100,000 departures, a reduction from 1984. The 17 total accidents (including nonfatal) represented an all-time record low.

For general aviation, the overall number of accidents, and the number of fatal accidents, declined as it has every year since 1978. In 1985, general aviation flew approximately *30 million hours.* There were 490 fatal accidents and 937 fatalities. The fatal accident rate was 1.53 per 100,000 hours, the lowest ever.

As far as foreign airlines go, many have extremely good safety records—some, perhaps, even better than ours. *Flight International* magazine analyzed world safety records in depth in its January 26, 1985, issue ("World Airline Safety Audit," by J. M. Ramsden). By the measure of fatal accidents per one million flights, 1973–84, the United States was ranked fourth behind (1) Australia, (2) Scandinavia, and (3) Japan. The United States, however, has a traffic volume larger than the other seventeen nations analyzed *combined.* Still, the safest countries according to *Flight International* audits over thirty years included (in alphabetical order) Australia, France, Japan, Scandinavia, the United Kingdom, the U.S., and West Germany, which is a nice thing to know if you're lucky enough to be traveling in any of those places.

And some countries, especially in Africa and Central and South America, have really scary (to me, anyway) accident records, but there are so many factors involved that to name names here, where a full analysis is impossible, would not be fair. If you're the intrepid sort likely to be found hopping on rickety air relics to traverse steaming jungles, I doubt you'd be daunted by a few statistics, anyway.

2. The Controlled Impact Demonstration (CID), conducted by an FAA and NASA team on December 1, 1984, was intended not only to test the new antimisting kerosene (AMK) that promises to reduce post-crash fires, but also to test a number of techniques for improving crash survivability and for investigating accidents. A Boeing 720 was specially wired and instrumented and flown by remote control to a carefully rigged desert site at Edwards Air Force Base,

where it was supposed to be crashed in the exact way most real crashes occur. In this, it succeeded perfectly: It crashed in a completely *unexpected* way. Despite extensive rehearsals, the plane came in at the "wrong" angle. Everyone had been looking forward to the final proof that AMK would minimize a fire. Everyone saw the test plane explode in a spectacular fireball. Actually, though, in some parts of the plane the AMK *had* worked, and beyond that, the investigators still gathered a tremendous amount of data about crash forces, the performance of experimental cabin furnishings and material, and the effects on the poor dummy "passengers," who were all heavily wired with sensors and whose ordeal was recorded on high-speed cameras (incidentally, as in most real crashes, the plane's structure remained relatively intact, and it was technically concluded that at least some of the "passengers" could have "survived" the CID crash—but of course, dummies don't evacuate very fast).

As for the future of AMK, some investigators maintain that, if the CID had gone as planned, the fuel would have been vindicated. Some investigators point out that crashes in real life don't go as planned, either. At any rate, the general consensus is that the experiment did not demonstrate conclusively that AMK does work, but neither did it prove that AMK *doesn't* work. There's a lot of pressure on the FAA to perfect AMK, since a fire-resistant fuel could probably save most of the lives that are lost in accidents. So stay tuned.

3. Dr. Daniel A. Johnson's book *Just in Case: A Passenger's Guide to Airplane Safety and Survival,* Plenum Press, 1984, along with the Flight Safety Foundation, were invaluable resources for this chapter. I think if I flew more than once or twice a week I would carry Dr. Johnson's book along with me. It is an *extremely* detailed guide (right down to where to step on the wing while you're evacuating), by one of the foremost authorities in the field, to the steps passengers can take to protect themselves in case of virtually any kind of conceivable emergency. Be sure and get your perspective in good working order before you read the book, though; after a couple of hundred pages of nothing *but* emergencies, you may start wondering why you've never been in one before. It may not be a book for fearful fliers, but it's certainly a book for careful ones.

CHAPTER SIX

1. For discussions of hyperventilation and panic attacks, see "Response to Hyperventilation in a Group of Patients With Panic Disorder," Jack M. Gorman, M.D., et al, *American Journal of Psychiatry,* July 1984; and "Hyperventilation as a cause of panic attacks," G. A. Hibbert, *British Medical Journal,* January 28, 1984. I found everything I ever wanted to know (and then some) about the incidence and physiology of airsickness in *Motion Sickness,* J. T. Reason and J. J. Brand, Academic Press, 1975. And thorough discussions of a wide range of medical issues related to flying are included in Dr. John H. Griest's comprehensive book *Fearless Flying: A Passenger Guide to Modern Air-*

line Travel, Nelson-Hall, 1981, whose estimate of the frequency of oxygen mask deployment I have used. Dr. E. Arnold Higgins of the FAA Civil Aeromedical Institute studied reported depressurization incidents over a ten-year period, 1974–83, and found about fifteen "significant" pressurization problems per year. I also appreciate information provided by Puritan-Bennett Aero Systems Company, manufacturers of aircraft oxygen and lighting systems.

2. I meant what I said about writing me. And to impress my publisher with my popularity, please do so at:

Layne Ridley
c/o *White Knuckles*
Doubleday & Company, Inc.
245 Park Avenue
New York, New York 10167

CHAPTER SEVEN

1. One of the most absorbing books I've ever read on *any* subject is *The Love and Fear of Flying* by Dr. Douglas D. Bond, International University Press, 1952, a study of emotional and psychological aspects of flying and combat, based on case studies of American and British World War II fighter pilots. I owe my appreciation of "High Flight" and its gallant author to this book, and to Hermann Hagedorn's biography of John Gillespie Magee, Jr., *Sunward I've Climbed,* MacMillan Co., 1942.